THE
CONTEMPLATIVE
TAROT

A CHRISTIAN GUIDE TO THE CARDS

BRITTANY MULLER

ST. MARTIN'S
ESSENTIALS
NEW YORK

First published in the United States by St. Martin's Essentials, an imprint
of St. Martin's Publishing Group

THE CONTEMPLATIVE TAROT. Copyright © 2022 by Brittany Muller.
All rights reserved. Printed in the United States of America.
For information, address St. Martin's Publishing Group,
120 Broadway, New York, NY 10271.

www.stmartins.com

Designed by Steven Seighman

The Library of Congress Cataloging-in-Publication Data
is available upon request.

ISBN 978-1-250-86357-7 (trade paperback)
ISBN 978-1-250-81091-5 (ebook)

Our books may be purchased in bulk for promotional, educational, or
business use. Please contact your local bookseller or the Macmillan Corporate
and Premium Sales Department at 1-800-221-7945, extension 5442, or by
email at MacmillanSpecialMarkets@macmillan.com.

First Edition: 2022

10   9   8   7   6   5   4   3   2   1

*For my grandfather, George, who showed me
how much curiosity a faith can hold*

CONTENTS

FOREWORD

By Carl McColman

Everyone knows social media is a mixed bag. We are all painfully aware of how online networking services contribute to political polarization or have provided a channel for the spread of misinformation and conspiracy theories. But there are real blessings and benefits associated with social media as well—from reconnecting with a long-lost friend from second grade to finding a group of people who share exactly your tastes and interests in art or fashion or whatever. Social media has also helped people with unique or distinctive spiritual values or practices to find one another. And so I felt such a rush of excitement when I first stumbled across Brittany Muller's Instagram feed, where she combines beautiful photography, including images from the tarot, with insightful meditations on the cards—all written from a clear Christian perspective.

Many Christians might wonder, "Why bother with the tarot?" and tarot enthusiasts might reply, "Why bother with Christianity?" But as Brittany Muller and her many thousands of followers can attest, there are plenty of us who find meaningful connections between our faith and the strange and wondrous symbolism found in the cards.

Take, for example, the Temperance card (XIV in the major arcana). This fascinating image presents an angel, red wings spread wide, an aura radiating around the being's blonde hair. Holding two large chalices, the angel is pouring water or some other fluid from one to the other—but it's pouring at a forty-five-degree angle, a physical impossibility. Likewise, the angel is standing with one foot on a stone and the other slightly submerged in a pool of water, but the angel's weight appears to be borne by the foot in the water—again, beyond the laws of ordinary physics. Surrounded by irises and a pathway leading to distant mountains before the setting sun, the entire scene feels like something from a dream.

Christians recognize *temperance* as a fruit of the spirit (Galatians 5:22–23), from a Greek word that means "self-restraint" or "self-control." It implies mastery or power over the self. But it also brings to mind the word *temperature,* which signifies the measurement of heat or cold, particularly in the human body; we take someone's temperature when trying to determine if they are sick or well.

So in a matter of minutes, this dreamy angel has encouraged me to consider how taking the measure of what is going on inside of me can be an important way of assessing my wellness—or lack thereof. Which brings me to why I, as a Christian, continue to study and appreciate the vivid and marvelous imagery of the tarot. It's a tool for getting to know my interior life, just like a thermometer or a stethoscope can aid a doctor in diagnosing ("knowing") what's going on in my body.

The images of the tarot tell a story. This has been called the Fool's Journey, from the card enigmatically numbered zero in the major arcana. I mentioned the pathway behind the angel of Temperance—it is one of many paths, roads, and other passages found in the seventy-eight images of a modern tarot deck. From the Eight of Cups to the Six of Swords to the Chariot in the major arcana, numerous tarot images evoke a sense of being on the move. I suppose it is a cliché to say life is a journey, but clichés exist because they point to something commonly experienced. We experience life as a journey because there *is* movement, in time if not through space. I am not the same person I was a decade or two ago, and neither are you: not only have nearly all the cells of our bodies changed entirely, but our very sense of self has adapted to new experiences, insights, and understandings. "You cannot step into the same river twice" applies as much to you as it does to the river. Yet while there might be a kind of temporal uniformity to the journey of life: we can expect to be a child for our first twelve years, an adolescent for the next six, a young adult for a decade or two after that, and so forth—there is also great variety: we all mature at different rates, age at our own pace, experience growth or decline, self-improvement or self-neglect in rhythms uniquely our own. The insights that enlightened you in college might remain hidden from me until I am elderly. So we are all on a journey, but what a rich, complex, and multivalent journey it is.

The seventy-eight images of the tarot seem to tell some sort of silent story, an almost mythic tale of its own. In this sense, the Fool is like Joseph Campbell's "hero with a thousand faces" and the tarot itself is like Gandalf or Obi-Wan Kenobi ushering Bilbo Baggins or Luke Skywalker into their own strange and life-changing adventures. But while we may watch *Star Wars* or read *The Fellowship of the Ring* to be entertained, the journey of the hero asks more of us: we are invited to bring our own journey into conversation with the strange and mystifying symbols we find in this deck of cards.

Christian interpreters of the tarot, from Valentin Tomberg and Mark Patrick Hederman to Brittany Muller, typically either ignore or reject the cards' reputed ability to predict the future. "Tarot for reflection, not divination" is how Brittany so succinctly puts it on her Instagram page. There is a very simple reason for this: Christians don't believe in fate. "The truth will set you free," promised Jesus, and we take him at his word. If I am free, then I do not have to break out in a sweat if the Tower card or the Ten of Swords shows up in a tarot spread. Which brings us back to the question of why bother with the cards at all. Brittany's distinction between divination and reflection is the clue to answer that question.

The seventy-eight images in the tarot are distinctive, unusual, ethereal, sometimes strangely beautiful, and at other times may seem unsettling or even disturbing. But if you've taken an honest look deep within yourself lately, you probably can recognize that there is remarkable beauty and unsettling stuff within your own heart, too. The journey of the Fool through the weird landscape of the tarot offers us a reflection on our own journeys, no matter how predictable or chaotic they might be. And because the tarot offers us images rather than lots of words, it bypasses the "watchful dragons" of the rational thinking mind and appeals directly to the hidden places deep in our subconscious.

This brings us back to the forty-five-degree-angle pouring of the Temperance card, which is one of several clues in the tarot that suggest these images are invitations into a dreamscape.

Truly, the tarot is reminiscent of a dream—a long, complex, and wondrously mystical dream. From swords to cups, knights to castles, angels to flowers, the images found in the cards seem sublime, meditative, otherworldly. Trying to interpret these cards can seem as daunting as trying to make sense of the uncanny logic and random reverie that visits you or me or anyone while sleeping. The best dream interpreters will encourage you to view your dream as a kind of deeply symbolic story you are telling yourself; there is no one "right" way to interpret the dream (as if symbols in our subconscious could only have one fixed meaning), but by having a kind of conversation with your dream, it can offer you surprising insights into the hidden places within your own psyche. The tarot can function similarly: a reflection, not of some immutable truth "out there," but of the liberating truth of the Spirit found poured into your very heart (Romans 5:5).

Why bother with the tarot? Because the cards invite us into a story, a journey, a dream, a mystery. The Fool, of course, is simply an alter ego for your or my or anyone's self. As Christians, this need not embarrass us; after all, Saint Paul invites us to be fools for Christ's sake (1 Corinthians 4:10). Jesus instructed us to become like little children (Matthew 18:3), therefore inviting us to be silly, to play, to wonder, and to laugh like the smallest ones among us. It's no accident that tarot originally was a game.

One more thing to say about Brittany Muller's wise advice: when we approach the tarot for *reflection,* it invites us to encounter these seventy-eight images through the practice of meditation and contemplation. It's no accident that the most renowned Christian commentary on the major arcana is titled *Meditations on the Tarot.* That book is densely philosophical, deeply esoteric, and difficult to read, but its basic message is sound: that these images can be profitably used by Christians for prayer and spiritual practice, leading to interior transformation. Meditation (reflecting on spiritual truth) and contemplation (resting silently in the love of God) are core Christian practices, dimensions of prayer and means for spiritual nurture. They are also the doorways to the mystical life, where "union with Christ" is more than just a theological principle, but a lived reality.

The Jesuit theologian Karl Rahner famously said half a century ago that the Christian of the future will be a mystic or will not exist. Is Rahner's future our present? Certainly, many people in our time have abandoned the liberating wisdom of Jesus Christ. Perhaps we cannot blame them for this, since the Christian church, institutionally speaking, has often been hostile to mysticism—just like the church has been unfriendly to the tarot. Perhaps there is a link between these tendencies of the church to be overly cautious—to the point, unfortunately, of quenching the spirit.

Many Christians reject that tarot because of its association with fortune-telling. Likewise, mysticism gets denounced for a variety of reasons: it is too pagan, too pantheistic, too eastern, too "new agey," too antiauthoritarian—all of these criticisms are patently unfair. I hope this book can not only help Christians discover a spiritually sound and helpful approach to the cards, but in doing so also contribute to the needed restoration of mystical spirituality within Christianity as well. In fact, Christianity has its own deeply rooted mystical tradition, and given the amount of Christian imagery found in classical tarot decks (like the Waite-Smith deck), it's reasonable to assume that tarot artists and commentators down the generations have recognized the deep affinity between the Fool's journey and the mysteries of faith that are encoded in the teachings of the great Christian mystics.

All this leads back to the question I imagined some tarot enthusiasts might ask: Why should those interested in tarot bother with Christianity? Without getting too lost in the details of Christian theology, I'll just say this: Christianity—at least, Christian mystical spirituality—offers a meaningful vision of a God who is love—pure, boundless, joyous love—and this vision invites us into a life transfigured by that divine love. Christianity invites us into a relationship with that God through Jesus, and through the Holy Spirit, through whom the love of God is poured into our hearts.

We live in what has been called the post-Christian age, so not everyone who picks up this book will identify as a Christian—just as not everyone who reads this book may have any prior knowledge of tarot. I think a lasting gift of this book will be how Brittany Muller plays matchmaker, introducing us to both the insights of the tarot and the splendor of Christian spirituality—and how they work together for anyone seeking that deep inner reflection that comes from the alchemical union of these two different yet related wisdom traditions. If you are new to either Christianity or the tarot, please set aside any preconceived notions you might have and approach the insights in the pages that follow with an open mind.

The great Christian mystic Julian of Norwich said, "the fullness of joy is to behold God in all." If we take this seriously (and I do), then we can behold God within us, embedded in our very souls—as we can also find God in a tool for soul exploration like the tarot. And we can meet God in the inner dialogue that emerges when we allow the images of the tarot to speak to our soul (and vice versa). I hope as you read Brittany Muller's thoughtful words, you won't just look for knowledge about the cards. Look for how the tarot invites you beyond itself, into the heart of divine love. And then take the journey—into the dream and into the mystery.

INTRODUCTION

Saint Augustine famously wrote, in the exquisitely personal voice of *The Confessions of Saint Augustine,* "Thou hast made us for thyself, O Lord, and our heart is restless until it finds its rest in thee." My own life makes the most sense to me when I view it through the lens of this same restless search. Here are the things that have pushed me away from God. Here are the things that have led me back to God. The things that push me away from God? They always seem easy and comfortable at first, but they leave me dissatisfied and restless. The things that pull me toward God? They are often difficult and demand more of me than I would like to give, but they bring peace with them, too. My whole life is an effort to remain keenly aware of the push and pull so as to find the resting place. It is an old struggle: Augustine wrote those words at the turn of the fifth century. It is a common struggle, too: the parable of the prodigal son is enduringly popular because so many of us feel compelled to live it for ourselves. But as Augustine says, we are made for God, and we can find rest.

I grew up in a Christian home. We were churchgoing but not settled about it, and I spent my young childhood hopping in and out of different Protestant denominations: Presbyterian, Methodist,

Southern Baptist. I saw spiritual restlessness firsthand. When I was thirteen, our family converted to Catholicism. In that steady tradition, my parents' restlessness ceased abruptly, and I picked up on their contentment. I spent my teenage years as a devout Catholic: regularly going to daily mass, spending time at adoration, reading theology for fun, acquiring a taste for God. It was a beautiful fledgling faith, but it's easy to be virtuous in the absence of temptation, and it's easy to have faith when nothing ever tests it. I became an adult and I left home and, embarrassingly, doubts pushed in almost immediately. Also embarrassingly, the doubts weren't even of an interesting variety. They were the same well-worn questions of faith that people have wrestled with for thousands of years. I didn't know how to be Catholic and also have doubts, and I didn't know how to be a Christian without being Catholic, and so I left everything behind.

I stopped reading Aquinas and Anselm and Augustine. I stopped going to church. I stopped praying. I simply disengaged from the questions I could not answer, distancing myself from anything having to do with religion and instead calling myself a "hopeful agnostic." The freedom was thrilling at first. It always is. I told myself that I could do what I wanted to do and believe what I wanted to believe and go where I wanted to go. But Christianity had been the thing around which my whole life was ordered, and I felt the absence of its gravity. I felt it particularly in my early twenties as I moved through the big life changes of marriage and children. By the age of twenty-five, I was living in Austin, Texas, with my husband (busy with law school) and our two sons under two (busy with keeping us awake at night). I was a stay-at-home mom, and I was struggling with the intensity of motherhood and the particular invisibility that often accompanies that kind of caretaking. I wanted something to anchor me, to order my days, to provide a rhythm to my life, to bring me back to myself. Where does one then turn when, before, one has always turned to prayer?

Austin has a reputation for being a "witchy" kind of place, and I found that reputation to be true. Most everyone I met was trying to cultivate some sort of personal spiritual meaning. I had friends who collected crystals, friends who practiced astrology, friends who went on Sunday morning hikes and called it church. I also had friends who played around with tarot cards. Captivated by the images, I bought a Waite-Smith deck for myself. I bought it because I was bored and restless. I bought it because I missed the intentionality of prayer. I bought it because I, too, was trying to cultivate meaning. Tarot scratched my itch for the ritual of religion, and I quickly fell in love with how it made me feel seen. I never used it for divination, because I've never believed in divination, but I loved creating a quiet space to shuffle cards and pull cards and sit with them. I loved getting to know characters like the Fool and the Empress, the Knights and the Queens. I loved registering my ever-changing reactions to these images and seeing myself, good and bad, reflected in them. Tarot helped me to know myself again. It was also a fine substitute for prayer, until it slowly became no longer the substitute but the substance.

The sneaky thing about tarot is that it is full of surprisingly Christian imagery. Tarot originated in fifteenth-century Italy, and the cards reflect the deeply Christian culture of that particular time and place. During a time in my life when I wanted nothing to do with Christianity—I simply refused to read Scripture or attempt prayer or darken the door of a church—I was pulling cards almost every day and using them mostly as journaling prompts. My Catholic upbringing wouldn't allow me to look past the Christian ideas that permeate the tarot. I would pull Temperance and write about the presence of that virtue in my life. I would pull the

Hierophant and meditate on the joys and sorrows of the institutional Church. I would pull the Devil and find myself reflecting on the nature of my own particular vices. Confronted with these images over and over again, I felt unable to escape my own sense of spiritual restlessness. Over the course of these years, my tarot practice began to feel less like a writing exercise and more like a prayer. The thing that had always helped me to see myself more clearly started to show me the God-shaped hole in my life.

I wish I had a dramatic story to tell about my return to Christianity, but the story holds no drama. I did not simply wake up one day and decide to believe in God again; my return to Christianity was as slow and meandering as my departure was sharp and abrupt. I admitted to myself that I missed religion, that I was restless and unsettled, that my own attempts at being "spiritual but not religious" were not enough. I quietly (almost furtively) started rereading some of my favorite spiritual writings from my teenage years: Augustine's *Confessions,* Henri Nouwen's *Life of the Beloved,* Teresa of Ávila's *The Interior Castle.* Living in Manhattan at the time, I wandered the medieval galleries of the Metropolitan Museum of Art and spent time with the religious art there. I popped into churches while out running errands and didn't tell anyone. I made fumbling attempts at prayer. I cried a lot. I also started attending an Episcopal church in our neighborhood at the request of my husband, who was looking for community after our move to New York City. We found ourselves going back every week, warmly welcomed by the people there. Slowly, almost imperceptibly, the restlessness went out like the tide.

This is the point in the story where the reader expects me to write about how I abandoned tarot in the peaceful wake of my return to Christianity. That would be a tidy ending, wouldn't it?

Tarot has a bad reputation, after all. I didn't abandon it, though. To be honest, the idea never once crossed my mind. It seemed unthinkable to me, because tarot was one of the things that led me back to God. To my mind, tarot and Christianity are a natural pair, even though their marriage seems strange at first (and second and third) glance. I integrated tarot seamlessly into my prayer practice, pulling cards with morning prayer and finding connections between the images and Scripture. To most everyone's surprise but my own, it fit perfectly. I was excited enough about this connection that I started to share my thoughts publicly, mostly on Instagram. A lot of people didn't like it. Tarot readers were suspicious of organized religion. Christians were suspicious of a practice tinged with the occult. But some people did like it. Enough people, at least, for me to be able to write this book for you.

Writing this book has been the greatest pleasure. I have loved being given the challenge of explaining tarot as a coherent, theological whole, and I have loved being given the gift of time to dive deeply into theology, time that I haven't had since I was a teenager. In looking for research and inspiration for this book, I drew from the theological sources that most move me: the early church fathers, the medieval mystics, the lives and writings of the saints, and many papal encyclicals. I spent the better part of a year reading Athanasius and Julian of Norwich, biographies on my favorite women saints, and slim volumes by popes on joy and suffering and mercy. (Reading this list of theological inspiration, you'll be unsurprised to learn that, while tarot led me back to Christianity, writing a book about tarot led me specifically back to Catholicism.) My research had a Catholic bent, and so the book has a natural Catholic bent as well. That being said, I've also tried to keep it as ecumenical as possible. While I read through a lot of specifically Catholic theology in researching this book, I also read through the Bible again, and in writing the book, I tried to draw from biblical common ground whenever I needed a story or a line of poetry or a feeling to illustrate the meaning of a card. In addition, I've used the NRSV translation of the Bible as it's the translation with which I am most familiar.

Writing *The Contemplative Tarot* has felt like a chance to write about the God whom I adore and the practice that taught me how to adore God again. For me, this book feels less like a how-to guide and more like a collection of seventy-eight little prayers. By that, I mean that these interpretations are my own and are deeply personal to me. I hope they will be helpful to you, but I also hope that you take them in the spirit in which they are given. They are not the rule of law. In most places I have tried not to stray too far from the original meanings of the cards, instead teasing out the theological implications of the traditional meanings, but what I tease out of the cards might be different from what you will tease out. Tarot's beauty lies in its ability to be constantly reinterpreted. What I hope, more than anything, is that this book will inspire you to slow down, to remain open to God's "still small voice," and to let the cards help you form your own prayers.

1

A BRIEF HISTORY OF TAROT

There are many histories of tarot; few of them are true. If you want to learn about tarot, you can read about how tarot contains the lost Hermetic knowledge of ancient Egypt. You can find intricate theories on tarot's esoteric connection to Kabbalah, that mystical Jewish school of thought. You can listen to arguments that tarot and the *I Ching* are intimately connected, being the major oracles of the West and East, respectively. You can learn about tarot's origins in Indian tantra and tarot's origins in Romani culture and tarot's origins in Waldensian teaching. There are as many theories on the beginnings of tarot as there are tarot readers to champion them, but these myths are just that. Elegant myths, never verified by the people who first espouse them, are taken for truth and become part of the culture of tarot. And so the history can appear murky, making tarot seem more mysterious than it is. Appearances are deceiving, though. In truth—in actual, verifiable truth—tarot began its life as nothing more than a card game with no purpose beyond providing entertainment to Italian nobles. This may be a disappointment for those who wish tarot to be more magical than it is, but if we follow the thread of truth, we find that the real history is interesting in its own right.

Renaissance Italy was nothing if not Catholic. How could it be anything else? At the time, the Catholic Church was undoubtedly the central institution of Western Christianity, and it was seated in Rome (apart from that brief and embarrassing detour to Avignon in the fourteenth century). The capital-C Church was in the Italians' backyard. In many ways, this was a point of pride, and of course Catholicism was a distinguishing mark of Italian culture. Much of the most famous art of the Italian Renaissance—Michelangelo's *Creation of Adam,* Leonardo da Vinci's *Last Supper,* Raphael's *Sistine Madonna*—is religious art. That being said, while this closeness to the Church was an inspiring gift, at times it was an equally inspiring point of revulsion. Sometimes closeness breeds contempt, and anyone who was that close to the institution of Catholicism had a front-row seat to the unsavory sides of the papacy not always apparent from a distance. While Petrarch was a devout Catholic, he had no problem lambasting the Curia, the administrative institution of the Church. Boccaccio's *The Decameron* contains stories that gleefully satirize the clergy. Dante's *The Divine Comedy* famously puts some popes in hell. The point is this: however one felt about religion, it could not be ignored. Good or bad, Christianity was a thing that had to be reckoned with.

Renaissance means "rebirth" and refers to the revival of classical antiquity that occurred first in Italy and then across the rest of Europe in the fifteenth century. What was being rebirthed during this time was interest in the ancient world. Works by Plato and Aristotle and Homer were brought back via the Italian trade routes that covered the Mediterranean. Scholars searched monastic libraries and found ancient manuscripts. There was a new blooming of interest in the Greek and Roman cultures of antiquity, and the thinkers of the Renaissance sought to revive the ideals of these cultures, to measure themselves by the standards of the ancient world, and to carry on its legacy. One of the intellectual challenges of the Italian Renaissance was figuring out how, exactly, to do those things. Obviously, much of what was being unearthed about the ancient world had its origins in pagan antiquity, and the people of fifteenth-century Italy self-identified as Christian to a degree that can be difficult for us to fathom today. Everything needed to fit, somehow, into a Christian worldview. This challenge was one of the sparks of the Renaissance. How could the pagan classics of antiquity and the Christian belief of the day be held together?

One of the men who wrestled with this challenge was Marsilio Ficino, a Catholic priest and dedicated scholar of Greek philosophy. The first to translate Plato's extant works into Latin, Ficino was deeply immersed in Platonic ideas, like the immortality of the soul, rewards and punishment after death, and a superior immaterial world that superintends the earthly world. If that sounds a lot like Christianity to you, you're not alone. Ficino was convinced that there were hidden depths in traditions not considered Christian—Platonism among them—that still aligned with Christian thought, and he worked to make that alignment clear.

While Ficino was trying to align pagan and Christian thought in his own philosophical way, the writers of the Renaissance were teasing out their own interpretations. This new acquaintance with classical antiquity familiarized the authors of the Italian Renaissance with allegory, a literary device that writers such as Petrarch and Dante used extensively to advance Christian thought. Dante's *Comedy* is a clear allegory for man's journey to salvation. Petrarch's

I Trionfi (Triumphs) evokes the Roman ceremony of the triumphal procession, honoring allegorical figures such as Love, Chastity, Death, and Time while showing us the ideal course of a man moving from sin to redemption.

Rooted in Christianity and enamored of pagan antiquity, ever trying to marry the two—this was the cultural environment that birthed tarot. The first tarot deck was created sometime in the early fifteenth century. We do not know exactly who it was created for, but the most likely candidate is Duke Filippo Maria Visconti of Milan. This new tarot deck would have been, in many ways, familiar to an Italian noble like the duke. Created not for divinatory purposes but for playing a game similar to bridge, it contained the four suits of the regular playing-card deck with which the Italian nobility would have been familiar: Cups, Batons, Coins, and Swords. These were pip cards, somewhat prosaic cards marked only with the small and standard symbols that denoted each card's suit and value. What made the new tarot decks special was the novel addition of a fifth suit consisting of twenty-one trumps and a Fool. These trump cards were originally illustrated but unlabeled, and while their symbolism and order varied among individual decks, their Renaissance influence was always clear. The trumps contained allegorical figures that expressed ideas from both Christian thought and classical antiquity. These are the same figures that are familiar to tarot readers today: Death, the Fool, the Empress, Temperance, Justice, etc. This is what tarot was from the start: nothing more than a card game with which Italian nobles could while away idle hours, and nothing less than an allegory for a journey through life.

So, what happened? How did tarot evolve from an unassuming card game to an esoteric divinatory device? It took a long time for that shift to happen. The game of tarot moved through

Europe over the course of several hundred years, but during this time it remained nothing more than a card game, and not even a particularly widespread one at that. Tarot died out in Italy. It remained fairly popular in France and Switzerland, but not really anywhere else. Eventually, tarot decks became standardized in the form of the Tarot de Marseille, a deck that is still in use today. At this point, however, it was still only a game. Tarot's shift from a simple card game to an occult tool shrouded in mystery happened not gradually but rather abruptly, and it happened in nineteenth-century France.

Napoleon Bonaparte was obsessed with Egypt. In his youth, he had been fascinated by the East and so, as an adult, he conducted a capricious military campaign in Egypt. The campaign had no real military purpose, but it got him close enough to the East for which he longed. In the true spirit of the Enlightenment of his time, he took a team of scientists and archaeologists with him on this campaign, ensuring that a steady stream of Egyptian artifacts found their way back to France. Because Napoleon was fascinated by Egypt, everyone in France was fascinated by Egypt. This curiosity snowballed into a fanatic infatuation with anything deemed "exotic" by the French. By the nineteenth century, many scholars began to seek out similarities between Christianity and other religions, such as Hinduism and Kabbalism. A renewed interest in the occult developed, and spiritual philosophies like spiritism, Theosophy, Freemasonry, and Martinism thrived. This was the beginning of the French occult revival, and it was in this atmosphere that tarot was transformed from a card game to a divinatory device. Removed from its Renaissance context, tarot became instead a mysterious object that appeared to contain promises of forgotten esoteric lore, rediscovered by people primed to find esoteric knowledge in everything.

The Protestant pastor and Freemason Antoine Court de Gébelin could be said to be the originator of tarot's connection to the occult. He lived in France in the eighteenth century, and while his interest in the occult predated France's occult revival, he set the stage for what tarot would become. The way Court de Gébelin told the story, he was once at a party in Paris where he came across some ladies playing the game of tarot. These cards were unusual in Paris, and he was struck by their imagery. Since he had what was, at the time, a precocious interest in the mysteries of ancient Egypt, his immediate thought upon seeing tarot cards was that the symbolism contained the remnants of the lost *Book of Thoth,* an ancient text supposed to have been written by the Egyptian god of writing and knowledge. With no reliance on either the historical reality of tarot or accurate knowledge of Egyptian hieroglyphics, Court de Gébelin took a mighty contextual leap and reconstructed tarot history. He made public his theories on tarot in an essay included in his work *Monde primitif, analysé et comparé avec le monde moderne.* In his hands, tarot lost its significance as a game and became something mysterious and wholly new. Court de Gébelin's new ideas on tarot later gained currency in Egypt-crazed France, with the help of one man.

While Antoine Court de Gébelin set the stage for the new tarot, it was Éliphas Lévi who brought tarot its full occult potential. Born Alphonse Louis Constant, Lévi originally pursued the Catholic priesthood and, after being ordained a deacon, abandoned the path to the priesthood at the age of twenty-six.

At the age of forty he began to publicly profess a knowledge of the occult and became an esotericist of great renown. He had a reputation as an original thinker, and his extensive writings on ceremonial magic attracted attention in nineteenth-century France. Lévi was also interested in the tarot, and he carefully incorporated the cards into his theories on magic. He believed, as Court de Gébelin did, that tarot contained within its symbols the secrets of ancient Egypt, and he used the images of the Tarot de Marseille to further his esoteric belief that *The Book of Thoth* was the origin of all religions. He did not, however, hold in high regard the idea of using tarot as a divinatory device. The use of tarot for divination had been familiar in France since the occultist Jean-Baptiste Alliette published, under the pseudonym Etteilla, a few small books about divinatory tarot in the late eighteenth century. Lévi knew of these books and believed that it was possible to use tarot for divination, but he also believed that tarot's most valuable purpose lay in its ability to convey ancient and universal wisdom.

As the nineteenth century drew to a close, there was a trend in France away from the use of tarot as a receptacle for universal wisdom and toward the use of tarot for divination. In response to this divinatory interest, the occultist Papus published *Le Tarot divinatoire: Clef du tirage des Cartes et des Sorts,* a tome dedicated entirely to cartomancy. While Papus himself did not have much respect for cartomancy, believing it to be primarily of interest to women, he had a thorough knowledge of tarot through his analyses of Lévi's work and was happy to capitalize on its interest. With Papus's work, tarot's transformation from a simple game to a complicated esoteric device was complete. Oblivious to the Italian origins of tarot, French occultists cemented tarot's place in the halls of the occult, successfully convincing the world that tarot was a mysterious Egyptian source of magical knowledge and a tool for divining the future.

It was during the French occult revival that tarot first became associated with esotericism, but interest in tarot didn't stay in France. Victorian England had its own occult revival sometime later, though it took on a different flavor there. The English had their own fascination with Egypt, of course, but they also developed a sort of fanaticism for Celtic culture, sparking the Celtic Revival, which so inspired writers like William Butler Yeats and AE Russell. By the 1880s, all manner of religious sects and spiritual groups were popular. The Counter-Enlightenment sparked the development of mystery cults like Freemasonry and Rosicrucianism, Theosophy and Swedenborgianism. Thanks to the new ease of reproducing books and pamphlets, many books on the occult came into wide circulation, including Lévi's writings on tarot. In the midst of all this spiritual renewal, tarot became a part of England's cultural milieu, and its emergence in English culture was helped along by one particular occult society.

The Hermetic Order of the Golden Dawn was founded in England toward the end of the nineteenth century. The founders—William Robert Woodman, William Wynn Westcott, and Samuel Liddell MacGregor Mathers—were Freemasons, and they founded the Golden Dawn in response to a set of documents called *The Cipher Manuscript*. Though there is much controversy surrounding the documents (among other theories, some believe they were written by Westcott himself in order to lend credence to the subsequently founded Golden Dawn), it is true that they formed the basis of the Golden Dawn's beliefs. *The Cipher Manuscript* gives an outline of a series of magical initiation rituals, contains information on magical theory, and offers a sort of magical curriculum that encompasses ideas relating to Kabbalism, astrology, alchemy, and tarot. The Golden Dawn's teachings drew from these ideas, connecting many of the esoteric threads of the day. As a result, the Golden Dawn became the crowning glory of England's occult revival. And though the order was small—it never possessed more than three hundred members—it had a mighty influence on the development of tarot.

It was the Golden Dawn that truly introduced tarot to England. One of the Golden Dawn's founders, Mathers, wrote the first guide to tarot in England, *The Tarot: Its Occult Signification, Use in Fortune-Telling, and Method of Play.* He published it in 1888, the same year the Golden Dawn was founded. This guide was really nothing more than a regurgitation of Éliphas Lévi's ideas on tarot, but, all the same, it established tarot in England as a magical tool and primed England for further ideas on tarot. This priming was useful for the members of the Golden Dawn, because they were busy taking their highly syncretistic system of magic and applying it to tarot, altering the sequence of the trump cards and linking tarot to the various mystical and magical interests of the day. At the time, all of this information was carefully guarded, because the Golden Dawn was exactly that kind of high-magic, highly secret society. Of course this information did not remain hidden. Everything was shrouded in mystery—until it wasn't.

The Golden Dawn had many famous members: Sir Arthur Conan Doyle, Charles Williams, Evelyn Underhill, William Butler Yeats, Bram Stoker. It also had one particularly infamous member: Aleister Crowley. Headstrong and astonishingly egotistical, Crowley advanced through the various levels of the Golden Dawn quickly. However, his morals and conduct were offensive to some members of the Golden Dawn, and he was eventually refused further advancement. Crowley retaliated by spilling the occult beans. In 1909 he published his book *Liber 777,* which gave to the world the Golden Dawn's secrets on tarot. He also started an occult periodical, *The Equinox,* in which he divulged garbled versions of the Golden Dawn's teachings. Crowley eventually left England, moving to Sicily and establishing the notorious Abbey of Thelema in 1920. Thelema was the name he gave to the spiritual philosophy he created from a mix of Golden Dawn teachings, yoga, and Eastern and Western mysticism. His teachings on Thelema inspired the later development of Wicca, and the tarot deck he created, the Thoth Tarot, is still in use today.

The history of tarot cannot be discussed without mention of Aleister Crowley. He made the Golden Dawn's secrets secret no more, divulging information that had an undeniable influence on modern tarot interpretations. However, the major innovator of tarot during this time was not Crowley, but Arthur Waite, a man less salacious but more renowned.

Arthur Waite was born in Brooklyn and grew up in England. He was raised a Catholic but also had an interest in the occult. As one might expect, this led to an eventual entrance into the Golden Dawn in 1891. Waite was never on good terms with the founders, though, and was dissatisfied with the Golden Dawn's emphasis on magic and the occult to the exclusion of mysticism. He left the Golden Dawn, rejoined it, became frustrated by the increasingly splintered infighting of the Golden Dawn's twilight days, and founded one of the handful of offshoots of the Golden Dawn. This offshoot, the Independent and Rectified Order of R. R. et A. C., disbanded in 1914. In 1915, he formed the Fellowship of the Rosy Cross, an organization that reflected Waite's interests in Rosicrucianism, Freemasonry, and Christian mysticism.

Waite was deeply immersed in tarot, and his influence on modern tarot cannot be underestimated. He spoke of the tarot symbolism as reflecting a mystic initiation and as a metaphor for spiritual rebirth. He believed that tarot did not contain occult truths but rather mystical ones. For Waite, tarot was less about gaining control of esoteric knowledge and more about connection with the spiritual life. Perhaps more than any other tarotist since the Italian Renaissance, Waite came closest to sensing the tarot's origins in Christian allegory. What's more, he was deeply immersed in Christian mysticism, and that immersion is evident in the deck he created. In 1909, Waite published his most famous contribution to the history of tarot, a tarot deck he created with the significant help of artist Pamela Colman Smith. What was special about the Waite-Smith deck was that while the trumps were illustrated, so were the pip cards. What was also special about the deck was that it standardized tarot's imagery. It became the most popular deck in the history of tarot, and almost every deck on the market today follows its templates of imagery and meaning. It is almost always the deck one sees in pop-culture images of tarot. It is most often the deck conjured in one's mind when tarot is mentioned. It is arguably the most easily recognizable tarot deck in the world. For those reasons, it is also the deck used in this book.

During the occult revivals of France and England, occultists were always in search of the one true tarot. They wanted to purify tarot, to bring it back to what they assumed to be its ancient Egyptian roots. They wanted tarot to unlock the secrets of the universe. They wanted to understand what they believed to be the ancient wisdom contained in tarot's images. These esoteric ideas about tarot began to shift subtly during the New Age movement of the 1970s. The New Age movement, in some ways, was not so different from the occult revival of the nineteenth century. There was a fanatical interest in "exotic" spiritualities. It became trendy to cherry-pick spiritual practices from Buddhism, Hinduism, Native American religions, and others. Things like astrology, crystal healing, and past-life regressions came into vogue.

It makes sense that tarot would become popular during this time, and it did. However, tarot was not used in quite the same way as it had been used before. The New Age was less focused on ancient universal wisdom and more focused on personal self-actualization. Tarot became less about learning the secrets of the universe and more about learning the secrets of the self. This shift from the universal to the personal was reflected in tarot's appearance. Beginning in the 1970s, there was a new wave of tarot decks on the market, each one suited to a special interest. The New Tarot contains a mix of Egyptian and Tahitian art. The Xultun Tarot attempts to fit ancient Mayan culture to the seventy-eight cards. The Morgan-Greer Tarot has a distinctly witchy feel. There was, and continues to be, a deck for whatever suits one's own spiritual and artistic preferences.

There has been a renewed interest in tarot in the last ten years or so, and the ways in which it is commonly used today have much in common with the New Age's focus on tarot as a tool for self-development. While tarot is still used for divination today among some people, it is more commonly used as a psychotherapeutic device. In my own experience, the people who read the cards today are less interested in magic and more interested in learning about and bettering themselves. These seventy-eight cards, which encompass such a wide range of human experience, can be used as a tool to facilitate inner knowledge, inner growth, and inner transformation. Their symbolism is a way to discern one's emotional states, to uncover thoughts and feelings one might be avoiding, and to create a quiet and meditative interior space. During a time when many people feel busy and pressured by the demands of modern life, tarot offers a way to slow down and look inward.

The history of tarot is a history of our search for meaning. The philosophers and artists and writers of the Italian Renaissance looked for meaning in classic antiquity and Christian theology. The occultists of France and England looked for meaning in ancient cultures, which they felt sure had answers they themselves did not. The tarot readers of the New Age movement looked for meaning in themselves. Tarot has been used as a card game, a receptacle for the mysteries of the universe, a tool for divining the future, a cheaper and more accessible substitute for therapy. But while the purpose of tarot has changed, its nature has not. Tarot is a vehicle for whatever it is we seek, and that is its particular and enduring gift.

2

WHY TAROT?

OUR CULTURE OF DISTRACTION

Many of us live in a world where it's possible—even easy!—to move through an entire day without a single second of quiet. We can check Twitter the moment we open our eyes in the morning, scroll through Instagram while we wait for our order at the coffee shop, listen to music during our commute, put on a podcast while we make dinner, and watch TV while we fold laundry before bed. We can pull out our phones while sitting at a red light, standing in line at the grocery store, or waiting for a friend at a bar. If there's ever a quiet minute, we always have in our hands the ability to fill it with noise.

Many of these diversions with which we fill our days are designed to be addictive, stimulating us to a fever pitch so we never stop scrolling. Even those of us who want to live more intentionally often have trouble resisting this allure, but when we spend all of our time consuming vast amounts of information, we have no space to reflect on what we're taking in. We become passive consumers, always focused outward and never looking inward, compulsively resisting any moment that would leave us alone with our thoughts, in favor of the small dopamine hit of feeling "plugged in." This kind of mindless passivity makes true self-reflection nearly impossible. To deeply know oneself is a holy thing, but how can we move into a deeper knowledge of the self if we're always training our focus on whatever keeps us from knowing?

Each age faces its own spiritual struggles, and the environment of constant distraction in which so many of us live feels like one of the defining spiritual struggles of our time. It is bad for our minds, but it is also bad for our souls. For those of us who wish to move more deeply into relationship with God, this noisy distraction can feel like a nearly insurmountable problem. How do we fight against the impulse of constant outward movement? How do we create enough stillness to hear the voice of God? How do we pray when every moment of the day offers us a chance to distract ourselves? These questions are important, because to live a life of constantly splintered concentration is to live a life in which it is extremely difficult to pray. If we are always running away from quiet, we are probably also running away from God.

For better or worse, this world in which we have distraction always within arm's reach is here for good. We know that this noise isn't going away. And while we cannot change this, we can find a better way to live in it. If we are to fight against the strong current of distraction, we need spiritual disciplines that can help us regularly disengage from the constant stimulation and reengage with a more contemplative frame of mind. We need a way to create space in our lives that will show us how to live more intentionally, with an eye toward something deeper and more nourishing. We need a tool that will help us to look at the self from which we so often run away and to quietly sit with it.

SLOWING DOWN AND MAKING SPACE

The desire to move toward a more intentionally contemplative way of life is reflected in the tarot's renaissance in recent years. In the last decade, tarot has made a reentry into popular culture, and it has done so in new and more expansive ways. No longer simply the domain of witches attempting to divine the future, these days tarot is as much a meditative practice as a divinatory one. To read tarot is to slow down, shuffle cards, look at images, sit in silence. Tarot demands an intentional focus in a way few things do these days, and it invites us into that focus.

Tarot is able to do this in part because it's so refreshingly analog. Most of us spend hours every day looking at screens, and this focus on digital technology can cause us to neglect the role our bodies play in our experiences of life. We can lose the kind of simple tactile experiences that have the ability to slow us down and pull us out of mindless scrolling and into the bodily experience of the present moment. One of tarot's greatest and simplest strengths is that it's impossible to shuffle a deck of tarot cards and hold a phone at the same time. To interact with something so material unhurries us. It sets our minds at a gentler speed. Pulling a single card and looking at it for even ten minutes, without looking at anything else, feels radical. It meets us right where we are and offers us a chance at a deeper seeing.

Tarot's ability to help us slow down and take a breath is a gift, but the true magic happens when this intentionality becomes a habit. To slow down once is nice; to slow down every day will change your life. It is in the ritual that we find real change, and tarot feels tailor-made for the ritual of slowness and space-making. It has the ability to create moments when, every day, we are quieting our hearts. And when we quiet our hearts, we start to notice things we had not noticed before.

SELF-REFLECTION

Today, tarot is most often used as a tool for self-reflection. When used well, it can strip away the layers of the external self, showing us what might be hiding underneath. To read tarot is to pull cards, look at the images, and ask oneself questions like "What do I feel when I look at this image?" and "Where do I see myself in this image?" and "How does this relate to my own life?" And then, most importantly, tarot prompts us to look unflinchingly at the answers. It's easy to dismiss this kind of self-reflective practice as unhelpful navel-gazing, but there's something to be said for taking the time to know oneself well. What's more, this practice is not mutually exclusive of prayer.

The pursuit of self-knowledge has a rich history in the Christian tradition, and it's often treated with a depth that isn't always found in secular ideas about the self. There are many examples of this, but my favorite is from *The Confessions,* the autobiography of Augustine's debauched youth and subsequent conversion to Christianity. There's a famous passage in *The Confessions* in which Augustine wrote about a particular instance during his adolescence when he stole some pears from his neighbor's orchard. Most of us would consider pear stealing to be a fairly venial sin, but Augustine scrutinized it mercilessly. He asked himself why he would steal pears when he had perfectly good pears of his own. He wrote about his feelings of eating part of a pear and then throwing the rest away. He thought about the company of boys he was with when he stole the pears and whether or not he would have done it had he been alone. It's a lot of reflection for what seems like a minor moment in Augustine's life. Augustine's deep commitment to self-knowledge is admirable, though, and it has something to teach us. There is no part of Augustine's soul, no matter how small, that escaped his inquiry, and he used his knowledge of self to reexamine his life through the lens of God's grace. Augustine's deep self-reflection gave him the ability to know himself more fully, but it also led him closer to the God he loved. In the Christian life, knowledge of self and knowledge of God are deeply intertwined.

John Calvin, in the opening pages of his *Institutes of the Christian Religion,* plays with this idea, writing that it is not possible to know God until we know ourselves. And this is true! We each must live with our own particular body and mind and soul, and to know our particularities is important inasmuch as they teach us about our specific gifts and how we can best relate to God. Calvin doesn't stop there, though. He turns this idea on its head, going on to write that we also cannot fully know ourselves until we know God, because it is God's goodness that reveals to us our need for God. Nearly every one of us has a deep, instinctive yearning for God, and it isn't until we acknowledge God that we are able to pinpoint that longing. Naming and interacting with that longing is also a part of honest self-knowledge.

These Christian ideas of self-reflection have a great depth, and it's because they have an end goal that pushes the self toward God. When interpreted through the lens of the Christian tradition, tarot can be used to this end, helping us to move into this deeper and more fulfilling kind of self-reflection. It has the ability to lead us closer to God through self-knowledge, because if we know ourselves more fully, we are more easily able to turn our hearts to God. By reflecting on the cards, we are able to examine more closely our own thoughts and feelings and then offer them in prayer. This kind of prayer, aided by the imagery of tarot, helps us to see our lives not just through our own human eyes, but also through the eyes of God. It helps us to pull into ourselves and then to move out of ourselves and into something bigger in a divine renarration of life.

VISIO DIVINA

A quick glance through the Bible is enough to show us that God speaks to his people through image. Jacob has a dream of angels ascending and descending a ladder. Moses has an encounter with God in the form of a burning bush. Peter goes to a rooftop to pray and has a vision of heaven. Jesus himself often explained his teachings using simple visual metaphors. We are a visual people, and images have the ability to touch our innermost reality, helping us to experience God in ways we can understand.

Visio divina is a Latin term that means "divine seeing." At its most simple, it is a prayer practice that involves praying with images. To practice *visio divina* is to gaze at an image with open eyes and open heart and to create a contemplative space in which one can feel the presence of God. It's a sort of affective mysticism, focusing on an experience of God that comes out of images and symbols, helping us to understand God in ways that can be felt with the senses. All contemplative prayer aims to encourage us to sink into the presence of God—to find God in all things—and *visio divina* is one way to do this.

Traditionally, *visio divina* has been used only with religious images. Because of this, it might seem strange to use tarot as a tool for *visio divina*. While tarot contains some religious imagery, it is not an explicitly religious tool. But a deck of tarot cards is nothing more and nothing less than a set of seventy-eight little works of art, and all art—even secular art—can lead us to God. God lives in all things and has the ability to speak to us through all beauty. The practice of *visio divina* is the practice of being moved by a work of art and entering into a moment of unspoken prayer with a God who wants to know us, and this can be done with tarot.

To use tarot in this more prayerful way helps us to look inward, not only to express our own authentic selves more fully, but also to know ourselves more fully in relation to God. Tarot allows us a space where we can look clearly at our emotions and figure out how they help or interfere with our connection to God. The practice of reflecting on these images can help us to reveal parts of ourselves that are difficult for us to see on our own. When used daily, a tarot practice can turn into a sort of examen—a daily spiritual self-review that allows us to reflect on God's presence in our lives. This kind of contemplation lifts our attention outside of ourselves in a truly meaningful way. It pulls us away from the shallow edges of life and into something deeper. In this way, tarot becomes a hunt for the true self and an exercise in finding God in all things, including our own lives. What is more contemplative than that?

3

HOW DO I PRAY WITH TAROT?

CHOOSING A DECK

A question I am often asked when discussing tarot and prayer is *What deck should I use?* There are hundreds of tarot decks being sold today—truly a deck to suit every taste—and the prospect of choosing one can be overwhelming. Because of that, and because the people asking these questions often want concrete answers instead of vague ones, I usually recommend the Waite-Smith Tarot deck. It is arguably the most recognizable tarot deck in the world. It was created by two Catholics, and while it is not an explicitly Christian tarot deck, I find the Christian symbolism to be more obvious than in other decks. Many of the tarot decks available for sale today use the Waite-Smith as a template, borrowing the basic symbolism found in its images. If you learn to read tarot using the Waite-Smith, it is easier to then branch out to other decks. While you can still use a different deck if you're learning to read tarot using this book, it will be easiest to use the deck I myself have used to write this book. The images of the cards you will find throughout the book are all from the Waite-Smith deck.

That's the easy answer. The more complicated answer is this: you need to decide for yourself what deck is best for you. If you like the Waite-Smith, that's lovely! If you don't like the Waite-Smith, there is truly no point in using it. To use tarot in a contemplative way is to marry prayer with art. It is to use the images of the tarot to facilitate intimate moments, and so the most important factor in choosing a deck is a connection with the art itself. You will not get anything out of the experience if you're forcing yourself to use the "right" deck and thus using a deck with which you feel no personal rapport. Ultimately, the best deck for you is a deck that you like, a deck whose images you feel excited to return to again and again. If you choose a different deck than the Waite-Smith, you will still be able to use this book and apply the meditations within it to the cards. Most tarot decks are structured in the same way and contain the same seventy-eight cards; they might vary in artistic interpretation but will not vary widely in meaning.

Many people I've talked with about tarot and prayer assume that in order to use tarot in a prayerful way, they must have a specifically Christian tarot deck. There are a number of Christian-themed tarot decks available for sale, and some of them are quite beautiful. If this is something you want, you can certainly find it, but, as evidenced by the deck used in this book, your deck doesn't need to have an explicitly Christian theme in order for it to be used in a contemplative way. In choosing a tarot deck, I feel that the best place to start is to think about what kind of art you like and then to buy a deck to suit those tastes. It might take time to find the right deck for you, and that's okay. Contemplation never rewards rush; there is plenty of time to take.

WAYS TO PRAY WITH TAROT

Teaching a person how to use tarot feels like teaching a person how to pray. Both are highly subjective; what works for one person might not work for another. My own journey with tarot has been intuitive and experimental, and I learned how to merge tarot and prayer by first and foremost remaining curious. I spent several years pulling a card every day and writing about it and thinking about it and letting it live in my heart. I returned to the cards again and again, slowly building a relationship that bore prayerful fruit. I think that the best way to learn how to pray with tarot is to do the same. Remain open to new things, be willing to be surprised and see what happens from there. That being said, tarot and Christianity is an unusual pairing of ideas, and guidance can be helpful. In the spirit of helpfulness, I'm offering you a few practical suggestions for using tarot in a prayerful way.

These are methods that I myself have used, and I encourage you to see them as interesting suggestions rather than the rule of law on tarot and prayer. Please do not feel as if you need to use only these methods in order to practice tarot "properly." You may choose to use the cards in this way; you may not. Because I'm Catholic, several of these methods stem from the traditions of the Catholic faith. If you come from a different religious tradition, I encourage you to be creative in merging tarot with your own faith practices. Tarot is deliciously open-ended. It begs to be used creatively. Give yourself the freedom to learn tarot the way I did, to play with the cards and to build a relationship with them. While I'm sharing some of my own prayer practices here, I have no doubt that you will find your own, and I can't wait to hear about them.

JOURNALING WITH TAROT

I bought my first tarot deck in 2015, on a whim. I bought it, in part, because I was mothering a newborn and a young toddler and I wanted some sort of intellectual project to balance the steady, unchanging routine of nursing and changing diapers and reading *Goodnight Moon*. I wanted something to think about, to hold in the back of my mind like a small treasure during slow, timeless days spent holding babies and not doing much else. I wanted to learn something new. So when I bought my first deck, I approached it as a project. I went through the deck in order, studying a different card each day. Because my approach to everything in life is to write about it, I wrote about each card as I studied it. I documented the traditional meanings of each card, meanings that I found in the little booklet that came with the deck but also on the many tarot blogs that are easy to find online. I also wrote about my own feelings on each card, whether they matched the traditional meanings or not. At the end of seventy-eight days, I knew every card, at least by sight, and I had a little book of meanings.

This is how I learned to read tarot, and I still think it's the best way to learn to do so. Seventy-eight cards is a lot of cards, and the process of familiarizing oneself with them can be overwhelming. If you need guidance in forming a friendship with them, I encourage you to take it slowly, focusing on one card a day (or even one card a week!) and taking ten or fifteen minutes to write down what thoughts or feelings come up in response to the image. If you need more structure than "write about your thoughts and feelings," I've included in this book reflection questions for each card that can guide your journaling. At the end of this process, I promise that you'll feel closer to the cards.

Journaling is a wonderful way to familiarize oneself with tarot, but it's not just for beginners. I never stopped using tarot in this way. I still pull a card most every morning in tandem with morning prayer (more on this later) and write about it. I have stacks of journals filled to the brim with tarot writing, and these journals feel like an intimate chronicle of my spiritual life. You might think that there's only so much a person can say about the cards, but that's not true. The revelations of the cards never end; they just change in texture. Through my journals, I can see how my feelings toward certain cards have changed through the years, how my theories on tarot have evolved and become more personal, and how the cards opened doors for me that would have otherwise remained locked. This is a deeply personal practice that I have carried with me through the years, and if you choose to carry this practice, too, I hope it serves you as well as it has served me.

TAROT AND DAILY PRAYER

If you are serious about your faith, then it's likely that you have some form of daily prayer practice. Maybe you're Episcopalian and pray morning prayer from the Book of Common Prayer each day, or you're Lutheran and pray each day from the Brotherhood Prayer Book. Or maybe you come from a less liturgical Christian denomination, and your daily time with God involves simply opening your Bible each day in faithfulness. Because I am Catholic, my daily prayer centers around the Liturgy of the Hours, the public prayer of the Catholic Church. While I rarely have time to pray all five of the daytime "hours," I always make time for morning prayer. Whatever our daily prayer practices, the point of them is to lead us closer to God, to keep us near to the heart of Christ, and to help us live in faithfulness. Tarot can work with these prayer practices, helping to deepen their meaning. Here's how that can work:

Begin by getting comfortable in the place where you pray, with your tarot deck and your Bible or prayer book. Shuffle your cards for however long feels right for you; a quick shuffle if you feel ready to pray, or perhaps a longer shuffle if you need time to slip out of the busyness of the day and into a quieter headspace. Then draw a card from the deck. Spend five minutes looking at the image on the card. This might feel like a long time, especially because the images of the tarot are small and usually simple at first glance, but they hide a lot of detail. Soften your gaze when you look at the card. We look at so many images every day that we have trained ourselves to only notice the most noticeable things, skating over finer details because our brains can only handle so much. But you are going to give yourself enough time with a single image to lovingly notice all the details. You are going to look carefully.

When your time with the card is up—when you feel like you've gleaned some feeling or meaning from the image—continue with your prayer. As you pray, keep your tarot card in your mind. Let its image lay over your prayer, highlighting things you might not have otherwise spent much time thinking about. If you sense connections, spend time contemplating them in prayer. Perhaps your card for the day is the Star, that archetype of stunning and vulnerable hope, and the Star helps you to notice the glimmering threads of hope in the psalms you read that day. Or maybe you pulled the Ace of Wands, an image of the gift of the Holy Spirit, and with that image in mind, you see in a Gospel story you've read a hundred times a flash of the Holy Spirit's fire that you had never noticed before. Used in this way, the images of the tarot can add a new dimension of thoughtfulness to your prayer, guiding you in ways you might not guide yourself.

I have noticed a tendency in myself to want to choose a card for this practice instead of pull one at random from the deck. I have tried it both ways, and I encourage you to let your draws be random. What I find most lovely about using tarot in this particular way is that it makes room for the surprising and unexpected. The way we live now is, in many ways, a very narrow way of life. Most of us spend a lot of time in online spaces, and the internet's algorithms, always trying to sell us something, are designed to only show us things we like. Pulling cards at random rather than deciding ourselves which ones deserve our attention allows us a chance to see things we haven't carefully selected for ourselves and to let ourselves be moved by them. If you pull a card that doesn't immediately resonate with you, sit with it anyway. Pray with it, and see if perhaps it just needed not to be rushed.

TAROT AND THE DAILY EXAMEN

One of my favorite devotions is *The Spiritual Exercises,* written by Ignatius of Loyola, a sixteenth-century Spanish saint. Ignatius was a single-minded man with a towering imagination and an equally towering intellect. He wanted, more than anything, to follow God's will, and he had a real vocation to teach others how to do the same. *The Spiritual Exercises* were written with that vocation in mind; they are meant to help others discern and follow the presence of God in their lives. *The Spiritual Exercises* are structured to be completed as an intense and immersive thirty-day retreat, but they don't have to be used in that way. (I myself have two children and, not having the capacity to step away from my life for a month, I have never used *The Spiritual Exercises* in this way.) Ignatius was a firm believer in praying as we can, not as we can't. He was a practical man, and he believed that *The Spiritual Exercises* should be adapted to suit the person trying to use them.

To that end, they contain a variety of different prayer techniques. One of the most well-known is the daily examen.

The daily examen is a technique of prayer that invites us to take a close look at each day in order to look for God's presence or perceived absence. Ignatius recommended that it be prayed at least once a day, usually in the evening. It is, like everything Ignatius did, clear and simple. To pray the examen, you begin by centering yourself and asking for illumination. Then you ask yourself two questions: What gave me life today? and What drained me of life today? You first look for gratitude, seeking God's presence in your life. You then look to the difficult moments, moments of weakness or moments when God felt far away. From these questions, you choose a feeling and pray on it. Perhaps God is directing you to gratitude. Or maybe God is directing you to meditate on a flash of anger in your day, a moment of weakness in which you fell away from God's will. At the end of the examen, you look to the next day ahead and ask God to give you help for the next day's challenges and gratitude for the next day's gifts.

The daily examen has been a part of my regular prayer practice for some time. For almost as long as I have been praying it, I have been using it in conjunction with tarot. In general, I don't like asking specific questions of the tarot. To do so leans a little too close to divination for my comfort, and I don't think that tarot is really for answering questions. I believe it works best when used as a tool for opening doors in our hearts, doors we might not otherwise notice. But I think that tarot works well with the open-ended questions of the daily examen. Each night, I ask God for clarity. I ask what gave me life today, and I pull a card. I ask what drained me of life today, and I pull another card. I've found that pulling cards for these questions often makes connections for me that I would not otherwise notice. For example, I might pull the contentious Five of Swords when asking what gave me life today, and I can thank God for the chance to practice soft-heartedness in a moment of argument. Or I'll pull the generous and giving Six of Pentacles when asking what drained me of life today and remember the person experiencing homelessness I passed by that morning without stopping to give a gift. I pray on the answers to those questions, and I ask God for help with the next day.

USING CARDS TO SET SPIRITUAL INTENTIONS

I grew up in a home filled to bursting with religious art. Being Catholic, my family had a crucifix in every room, holy-water fonts scattered through the house, and the mandatory statue of Mary in the front yard. I always liked this, because I like religion, and being surrounded by religious art had a way of drawing me into the spiritual life. I was never able to forget my faith, because reminders lived in every corner of my family's home. As an adult, I've adopted my parents' same attitude toward religious art. The tarnished silver Sacred Heart hanging by the kitchen reminds me, each time I pass it, to be more openhearted. The votive candle for Saint Michael the Archangel in my bedroom reminds me of the protection I have in the life of faith. Crucifixes keep the brutally compassionate love of Christ ever present. In the entryway, right by the front door, hangs a large print of Our Lady of Guadalupe, a greeting from my heavenly mother as I come and go each day.

It makes sense to use religious art to set spiritual intentions for oneself, to serve as reminders of faith. And in the last year or so, I've started doing this with tarot cards as well. I have a small card holder on the bookshelf in my bedroom, near my crucifix and my icon of Our Lady of Perpetual Help. In that card holder, I keep a tarot card propped up. It's not one that I've drawn at random, but one that I've chosen for a specific reason. Right now, the card

I have displayed is the Sun. As I write this, it is Advent, and each time I look at this card, it draws my mind to thoughts of the Incarnation and the birth of Christ and the physical presence of divine love. When I feel that it's time for a change, I'll decide on a new card.

One of my favorite things about tarot is how malleable it is. It can be used so well for so many things. In this chapter, I've given you some examples for using tarot that work best when drawing cards at random, and I think that there is a spiritual advantage to that. I also think, though, that there are useful spiritual practices which involve choosing cards with intention and care, as I've done with my own cards. I encourage you to play with this idea. As you read through this book, if there's a card that strikes you as particularly relevant to your current spiritual life, prop it up on your bookshelf or keep it on your nightstand for a while, or use an image of the card as the lock screen on your phone. Make it something you see every day, and see if it changes your heart.

WORKING WITH MULTIPLE CARDS

When I first started playing with tarot, I spent several years pulling just one card a day before I ever experimented with spreads of multiple cards. And even then, for some time after that, I would only look at pairs of cards, finding common ground or interesting tension between different duos. These days my tarot practice most often involves drawing a single card. This is because I like to keep things simple, but it's also because I'm a mother to young children and my time to pray is usually limited. If I pull multiple cards, I often find that I don't have the time I need to give them fruitful attention. That being said, if I have a longer stretch of time to pray (say, for example, if my kids are sleeping late one morning, or if my husband has taken them to the park for the afternoon and the house is quiet), I might pray in one of the ways I've shared in this chapter, but drawing two, three, or four cards instead of one.

Tarot is not a set of seventy-eight unconnected images. It is a system, and the cards can play off and play with each other in surprising and fruitful ways. I liken this to the way different passages of Scripture marry well together. Every time I go to mass I hear readings from different parts of the Bible: a reading from the Old or New Testament (or both), a Psalm, and a reading from a Gospel. Hearing these passages read together can create connections I might not otherwise notice. Tarot works in the same way. Pulling the High Priestess in conjunction with Strength teases out its more contemplative aspects in ways I might not otherwise notice. The Devil followed by a card like the Five of Swords or the Seven of Wands prompts me to contemplate the presence or absence of vice in those images. Looking at the fiery Knight of Wands next to the gentle Queen of Cups invites thoughts of how these two personalities might work fruitfully together. There are an infinite number of visual connections between and among the various cards. As you become more comfortable with tarot, learning meanings and gaining familiarity with the images, this is the natural next step on your journey. Experiment with drawing multiple cards for the prayer practices included in this book or any prayer practices you may invent yourself. Play with them and see what they tell you.

4

THE MAJOR ARCANA

A tarot deck can be split into two parts: the major arcana and the minor arcana. The term "arcana" comes from the Latin word *arcanus,* meaning "secret." The major arcana consists of twenty-two cards, each with a number and a name. The cards of the major arcana are the cards most often seen in popular depictions of tarot. These are the famous cards, cards like the Fool, the Tower, Death, and the Wheel of Fortune. They represent archetypal figures and situations, and because of that, their meanings are often more complex than the cards of the minor arcana. More allegorical than the rest of the deck, the major arcana tells us about big-picture ideas. It invites us to reflect on things like the cardinal and theological virtues; the Four Last Things of Christian eschatology: Death, Judgement, Heaven, and Hell; and the nature of God. The major arcana gives us space to pull back and reflect on our lives from a broader perspective, to give mental and spiritual weight to the more dramatic moments of our lives: love, birth, death, change. These cards remind us that, while we each play but a small part, we are each intimately woven into God's great story. We are connected to something bigger than ourselves, and that's worth paying attention to.

THE FOOL

Do not deceive yourselves. If you think that you are wise in this age, you should become fools so that you may become wise. (1 Corinthians 3:18)

Every tarot deck starts with the Fool. A young person, having stripped himself of worldly attachments, is about to joyfully step off a cliff to fall into the abyss of God. Our Fool is a Holy Fool, and the Holy Fool is characterized by complete abandonment to God. This is why the Fool, in a tarot deck, is represented by the number zero. He has no identity outside the love of God. He rests on the idea that to become closer to God, we must relinquish all knowledge and all power and all pride. We must let go of everything we think we need, everything we think we want, everything we think we know.

Because the Fool belongs to God so completely, he has no worldly power. He has placed himself outside of worldly ideas of success, simply removing himself from the world's competition and choosing a different path. The Fool's life is a life lived on the margins. It is a deliberate flouting of social conventions and a seeking of God where others would never think to look. It is radical humility and simple holiness, what the world calls weakness. Because of this, the Fool is a sort of prophet. He functions as a check on our own obliviousness or arrogance, holding up a mirror to our hardened hearts. He points to our self-important and ambitious natures and reminds us that it is dangerous to take ourselves too seriously. To experience God is to become foolish in the eyes of the world, but the Fool knows that this is no loss.

The Fool gives up not only worldly ideas of success, but also his intellectual power. He does not do this by completely abandoning his intellect, but by placing it in service to God. He recognizes that his intellect can only take him so far, that in order to become closer to God we must let go of any hope to ever fully know him. The intellect is silent in the presence of God, and the Fool is comfortable in this silence. He lives in it, in the liminal space between human will and intellectual servanthood, balanced on sheer faith and learning to desire something more of God than simple knowledge of God. The Fool attempts to turn us away from our intellectual piety and toward something more mysterious and more difficult to grasp. He asks us not how clever we are, but how merciful. He asks us not how proud we are of ourselves, but how humble we are willing to be before the God we claim to seek.

This worldly and intellectual simplicity—this unselfconsciousness —gives the Fool a childlike quality. There is a joy and a lightness in the Fool. This relinquishing of power is not cynical or nihilistic. It's a sort of poetic, naive courage. To embody the Fool is to come to the edge of life and then to open one's hands, with wild abandon, for yet more life. Those of us who wish to love God better often take our faith journeys very seriously, and the Fool instructs us otherwise. We are children in the eyes of God, and we should be able to laugh at ourselves, at how little we know about God and how we choose to seek God all the same. This childlike trust of the Fool, this turning to faith, is not where a theoretical journey to God ends (as if it can ever end). It is, rather, where it begins—with a relinquishing of power and pride and then a faithful leap into the unknown and unknowable. This leap off the cliff is a tumbling into a journey from which we cannot return. The Fool stands right on the edge, yet there is no terror, only joy.

REFLECTIONS

- What are you holding on to that keeps you from fully seeking God? Is there anything that holds you back?
- In what ways can you bring more Fool-like playfulness into your life? How can you take yourself less seriously?
- How do you define success? What does a successful version of you look like? How does your definition of success align with the love of God?
- What in your life would need to change for you to feel brave enough to jump off the Fool's cliff?
- How can you cultivate the Fool's humility in your life of faith?
- In the journey to know God more fully, intellect can only take you so far. What other ways of knowing can you seek?

THE MAGICIAN

But you are a chosen race, a royal priesthood, a holy nation, God's own people, in order that you may proclaim the mighty acts of him who called you out of darkness into his marvelous light. (1 Peter 2:9)

At the heart of religious devotion is wonder. Wonder, true wonder, is what happens when a person sees God in someone or something and feels compelled to take off her proverbial sandals and kiss holy ground. It's the kind of powerful awe that urges a person to life-changing action, the desire to reach out and touch the sacred. The Magician lives his life in search of this wonder. He knows that the world is full of religious feeling if one bothers to look for it, and look for it he does. Centered between heaven and earth, one hand pointed up and holding a wand, and one hand pointed down, he shows us how to bring them together so we, too, can see the world as charged with golden beauty. Crowned with a lemniscate, that symbol of eternity, he shows us how to find the eternal in the everyday and the magic in the ordinary. He reminds us that we are called to this, too.

On the Magician's altar are laid out the four symbols of the four suits of the minor arcana: wand, sword, pentacle, and cup. These items are objects of ritual. While they are perfectly ordinary objects, they also symbolize the Magician's effort to find the wonder of God in every unassuming nook and cranny of the world. They're reminiscent of the Christian sacraments, tangible signs of the invisible graces given to us by God. The sacraments—rituals like baptism and the Eucharist—are channels for God's grace, physically representing the gifts we receive from God. They charge our lives with meaning and remind us that grace is ours to reach out and touch.

The Magician has his ritual tools, but he has something else, too. This image is framed by lilies and roses, an abundance of almost overgrown greenery. While the Magician's tools are helpful in his pursuit of religious wonder, man-made objects do not provide the only way through which he experiences the wonder of God in the world. God made the world to give himself to us through his creation, and the Magician, surrounded by the lushness of nature, knows this. He knows that all things are made by God, and so all things have some sense of sacramental depth. God made everything and declared it good, and everything is touched by the sacred. The tarot's Magician wants us to know that it is possible to experience God in all sorts of ways, whether through our own religious rituals or through God's own creation. Wonder can be found anywhere.

The ritualistic way in which the Magician interacts with the physical world is reminiscent of the priesthood. To be a priest is to be courageous enough to stand between heaven and earth and to dedicate one's life to religious wonder, as the Magician does. There's an instinct to associate priesthood with power, to assume that one must be specially called to seek wonder with such fervor. The Magician says otherwise. His pose is open, and he looks directly at us, inviting us into the scene. The goal of priesthood is service, and that is the task of the Magician as well. He is devoted to a religious ideal, and he wants to spark in us that same devotion.

The nature of wonder is that it wants to be shared. The Magician has a great desire to guide us into a connection with the spiritual world in order to keep the soul—the magic—of religion alive. We, in turn, share that wonder with others. We are not all ordained priests, but we are God's own people. Wonder is our birthright, and we are all called to the Magician's task of religious devotion, of finding God in the world. It is our duty as well, and our delight, to find that golden wonder in all things. In doing so, we lift the whole world into the miracle that God proclaims it to be.

REFLECTIONS

- Reflect on your own experiences with religion. Do you feel like religion has instilled a sense of wonder in you? Why or why not?
- Have you ever had a moment of religious wonder? How did it change you?
- Who in your life has been a Magician for you, guiding you to wonder?
- How can you be a Magician for other people? How can you guide others to their own sense of wonder, their own experiences of God?

- Where in your life do you feel closest to religious wonder? In beautiful churches? At the edge of the ocean? In the presence of your family? (There are no right or wrong answers!)
- Do you see yourself in the Magician? Why or why not?

THE HIGH PRIESTESS

I want their hearts to be encouraged and united in love, so that they may have all the riches of assured understanding and have the knowledge of God's mystery, that is, Christ himself, in whom are hidden all the treasures of wisdom and knowledge. (Colossians 2:2–3)

If you are reading this book, it is likely that you have an interest in the contemplative life. It is also likely that you already know how difficult the contemplative life can be. It is easier to *do* than to *be*. It is easier to move than to sit still. It is easier to distract ourselves than to quiet our minds. Most of us lead busy lives, and excuses are easy to come by. For these reasons and many others, the contemplative life can sometimes feel unattainable. The High Priestess, wrapped in her serene mantle of silence, insists that it is not. Like Mary, who "treasured all these words and pondered them in her heart" (Luke 2:19), the High Priestess is a true contemplative. She has the knowledge of God's mystery; she wants us to have that knowledge, too, and so she guides us to the place of interior still- ness that she herself possesses, the place in which the mystery of God can be encountered.

For the High Priestess, contemplation is not some sort of fuzzy meditation, a vague emptying of the mind. The High Priestess isn't contemplating nothing. The stillness and silence of the High Priestess is rooted in Scripture and in the life of Christ, and this is evident in the symbolism of the Waite-Smith depiction. The B and J on the High Priestess's columns stand for Bethlehem and Jerusalem, the respective birthplace and death place of Jesus. The High Priestess holds a scroll, a representation of Scripture. The pomegranates behind her are traditional symbols of the Christian Church. On her breast, in the very center of the image, is the cross.

The Christian imagery that surrounds the High Priestess is important. It's important because what we see behind the High Priestess is not a church or a temple but a vast ocean. In the con- templative life, what we are opening ourselves up to is not the knowable God but the unknowable God. We are diving into mystery itself. Because of this, it's helpful to have a religious tra- dition to use as a sort of guide into this mystery, and the High Priestess knows this. She sits before this inexhaustible ocean as the gatekeeper. With the moon at her feet, she reminds us that in con- templative prayer we enter into the dark mystery of unknowing. With the cross at her breast, she reminds us that the mystery is, as Colossians says, Christ himself.

The imagery of the Waite-Smith High Priestess borrows heav- ily from traditional personifications of the virtue of faith. This is what the High Priestess is really about. While faith seems like a plain and simple idea, that simplicity hides great depth. Faith, at its core, is about the acceptance of mystery. It is about feeling certain of what is known, and comfortable with what is unknown. That acceptance of what is unknown can be so difficult, because we so badly want certainty. It can feel unbearable not to know the things we want to know, but to be a Christian is to wrestle daily with mystery. We can enter into God through what Julian of Norwich called "mysterious touches," but we can only receive what little our minds can bear. The High Priestess teaches us how to accept those mysterious touches. The luminous vastness of God is available to us, and the High Priestess can guide us there, teaching us to ground ourselves in tradition and listen faithfully in silence.

REFLECTIONS

- What distractions come up for you when you try to pray? Worries? Frustrations? To-do lists? How can you let go of those distractions, even for a short time?
- The contemplative life of the High Priestess is rooted in religious ideas. Do you feel as if your own religious practices aid you in contemplation? Why or why not?
- Reflect on the idea of an unknowable God. Does this make the idea of contemplating God feel pointless for you? Or like a great adventure? Why?
- Reflect on the definition of faith found in Hebrews 11:1—"the conviction of things not seen." How do you think the High Priestess might help you cultivate that in your spiritual life?

- Do you feel more comfortable approaching your relationship with God from the perspective of feeling or of logic? Why?
- How much silence do you encounter in your day-to-day life? How can you build more silence into your days?

THE EMPRESS

Yet it was I who taught Ephraim to walk, I took them up in my arms; but they did not know that I healed them. I led them with cords of human kindness, with bands of love. I was to them like those who lift infants to their cheeks. I bent down to them and fed them. (Hosea 11:3–4)

The entire universe—all we know and all we don't—has been lovingly created by the God who adores us beyond all understanding. It has all been set down precisely for us, with great care and devotion, for our pleasure. This creative and abundant divine love is what we see represented in the Empress. The Empress shows us God as the infinitely nurturing Creator, the God who made us and the God who made everything else. This is the God who brings forth the world for us, labors over it, births it through patient endurance, and offers it as a gift to us. Through the archetype of the Empress, we glimpse a God whose energy is constructive rather than destructive, a God whose aim is to show us how much pleasure God has to give. Crowned with stars and surrounded by the glory of a creation made for us to enjoy, the Empress shows us a God whose greatest wish is that we delight in all she has made for us.

This creative and nurturing energy we see here is, at its heart, a maternal energy. We are familiar with the idea of God as Father, but God is also Mother, and the Empress plays with this idea of God's maternal love. The Empress sits in the very middle of her creation. She is not at all removed from it. In positioning herself in this way, she reminds us that God did not create the world and then leave us to it. Like a good mother, God broods over the world. Like a good mother, God is always close to her children. Having given us our very being, of course God is bound to stay with us and to care for us. We can rest like children in the gentle fact of God's eternal presence. Indeed, we are called to a childlike, instinctual trust in the perfect maternal love of God, and the Empress, in reminding us of God's maternal nature, invites us into this kind of love.

Beside the Empress sits a stone engraved with the symbol of Venus, goddess of love and beauty. The Empress reminds us that God is our Mother; she also reminds us that we are allowed to take pleasure in the gifts of God's creation. She is surrounded by a lush landscape: cypress trees to sit under, a flowing river to splash in, an abundant wheat harvest to keep our bellies full. We are allowed this abundance. We are allowed this beauty. We are allowed to enjoy this life. God does not offer us the world begrudgingly. God made the world for us, and there is beauty here, and it is for us. We are the apples of God's eternal eye, and God wants to lift us to her, to hear us laugh in pleasure, and to watch us play in the world she has made for us.

Many of us have grown up with ideas of God as omnipotent judge, God as stern Father, God as unknowable mystery. These ideas of God are all correct; nothing contains more multitudes than God. But God is also this: a mother who loves her children and wishes joy for them. The perfect maternal love of God demands nothing but that we accept it. All we have to do is open our hands to it. We can connect with God through this pleasure and this beauty, through the enjoyment of God's creation. As God's children, we are made by God with God's maternal hands, and we can allow ourselves to be mothered by accepting the gifts that God gives us. There is a reason that it feels good to climb a tree, to swim in a river, to eat an abundant meal. It's because it connects us with God our Mother, always wanting a loving connection with us, always wanting to hold us to her cheek, always wanting to bend down and feed us.

REFLECTIONS

- Reflect on the idea of God as Mother. Does it feel comfortable or uncomfortable for you? Why?
- In what specific ways can you take simple pleasure in God's creation today? Can you see that pleasure as an act of praise?
- Like a good mother, God is close to us always. Does that kind of watchfulness feel good to you? Why or why not?
- In what ways can you bring a childlike trust into your relationship with God? How can you more fully trust in God's benevolence and love for you?

- Reflect on the words of Christ in Matthew 23:37—"how often have I desired to gather your children together as a hen gathers her brood under her wings, and you were not willing!" Have you ever felt unwilling to accept God's maternal love? If so, why?
- Spend some time thinking about your own associations with mothers and motherhood. How might those associations color your feelings about God as Mother?

THE EMPEROR

Those who trust in the Lord are like Mount Zion,
which cannot be moved, but abides forever.
(Psalm 125:1)

God is merciful and loving. God is also bigger and more powerful than we can understand. These things are not mutually exclusive. The Emperor represents God as eternal and mighty, the Ancient of Days. Ancient of Days is a biblical title for God, which comes from the book of Daniel, and it emphasizes God's aspects of omnipotence and omniscience. To be the Ancient of Days is to know all and to be all, and we see this power in the symbolism of the Waite-Smith Emperor. He holds a golden sphere—a symbol of the world—in the palm of his hand. He holds court in the open air because the entire universe is his kingdom. The Emperor reminds us that God's vastness is more than we will ever know. He dwells without beginning or end. We and everything we know live under his gaze.

There's a certain grandeur in the kind of stability that the Emperor represents. If God is eternal, then God exists outside our notions of time. Indeed, he holds time itself in his hands. It's difficult for us to conceptualize this limitlessness of God, but the mountains behind the Emperor help us to inch closer to the idea. Mountains are not truly eternal. They do rise and fall, but they do so on such a grand scale of time that they seem nearly permanent to our human conception. These natural processes that occur over eons—the formation of mountains, the carving out of canyons, the growth of forests—these are things that happen so slowly that they can feel eternal to us, even if they aren't. The Emperor, and the mountains behind him, help to pull us into a different scale of time, one that is closer to eternity than our own short lives. That limitlessness, the ungraspable scope of it, is where God works. That scale of time can be scary, but there's also something very reassuring about this kind of eternity. It doesn't go anywhere. Like a mountain, you can throw yourself on it and it will hold you.

The eternal and unchanging nature of God can hold us, and that is a comfort. What is sometimes less comforting is our weakness in comparison with God. We sometimes like to make God smaller than he really is in an effort to grasp him, and it can be difficult to wrestle with the idea that God is beyond our power to control. God does not and will not change for us. In comparison with God's eternal nature, we are utterly small and weak. We can barely even begin to understand God, much less change God in any way. Because we are incapable of controlling the nature of God, we have to learn to trust God instead. We have to let God to be bigger than us. We have to allow God the authority that is his due.

The Emperor shows us God's immense authority. He also shows us the way in which God wields it. The Emperor is a figure of supreme authority, but he holds no weapon. God rules by the scepter, not by the sword. His power lies in giving his power away, because true power is always the renunciation of power. God is a God of love and mercy. He does not rule by violence, because he does not need violence. God rules only by the intrinsic authority of the divine—by truth and beauty and goodness. This is what is so radical about the authority of God: it is based not on a will to power, but a will to serve. God sits in solemn and eternal state, but he also sits in rest and in peace. His power is rooted not in force but in an endless capacity for giving. If we can manage to internalize this, it becomes much easier to trust in God. We can learn to relax in his eternal nature rather than struggle to make it smaller than it is. We can trust that Mount Zion will stand forever.

REFLECTIONS

- What aspects of God's creation help you feel connected to the vastness of God? What about them calls to mind that vastness?
- Spend some time meditating on the nearly inconceivable expanse of God. Does it feel comforting for you? Or does it make you uneasy? Why?
- Do you ever find yourself trying to control God's narrative, to make that divine vastness somehow containable? If so, how can you let go of that control and shift into faith instead?

- Do you feel as if it's easy to trust in God's power over you? Why or why not?
- Has there ever been a moment when you felt in touch with a more eternal concept of time? What did it feel like?
- Reflect on the power and privilege you have in your own life. How can you give it away to make space for more love and mercy?

THE HIEROPHANT

So then you are no longer strangers and aliens, but you are citizens with the saints and also members of the household of God, built upon the foundation of the apostles and prophets, with Christ Jesus himself as the cornerstone. In him the whole structure is joined together and grows into a holy temple in the Lord; in whom you also are built together spiritually into a dwelling place for God. (Ephesians 2:19–22)

Everyone has moments in their lives when mystery strains at the seams of ordinary life. These moments of small miracles charged with meaning—a wedding, the birth of a child, a special encounter with a work of art—are times when we feel pulled out of the smallness of our own lives and into a part of something bigger. It's natural to want to hold on to and make sense of these moments, and the Hierophant helps us to do so. The word "hierophant" is from the Greek *hieros,* meaning "sacred," and *phainein,* meaning "show" or "reveal." A hierophant is a person who interprets sacred mysteries, who reveals the sacred for us. The tarot's Hierophant speaks to our desire to make sense of those mysterious moments we happen upon in our lives. He recognizes our desire to experience more depth in life, to feel that there is something more than the mundane.

This desire to inquire into the deeper meaning of things is an innately religious one, and the Hierophant of the tarot is particularly associated with religious tradition and the way that structured religion (as opposed to a looser kind of spirituality) can help us to reveal holy things. A hierophant is a revealer of mysteries, but the tarot's Hierophant doesn't just pull back a curtain to reveal the open face of God. What he does is offer us a religious tradition that gives us a key to unlock divine mystery. Religion can give us a language to explain the pieces of our lives for which we have no other words. It's an inadequate language, to be sure, because God is beyond language, and mysteries are mysteries for a reason, but using language that is lacking is better than using no language at all. It's a gift to have others' prayers to fall back on when we can't make our own.

Religion offers us a language and a structure in which to explain spiritual moments in our lives. It also gives us a community of shared beliefs. The Hierophant is a symbol of the gifts we receive from being part of a communion of believers, and the obligations that derive from respecting one another. To be a part of a Christian community is to care for others and to be cared for by others, to bless and to be blessed, as the Hierophant blesses the priests in front of him. The gift of this is that we can connect with God by connecting with other people, and we can become closer to God by caring for those around us. A religious tradition can give us a space to be vulnerable, to share those mysterious moments with people who will respect them for what they are, and to affirm those moments for others. It's another way of revealing the sacred.

The Hierophant shows us what religion, at its best, can do. It can offer a benediction for our entire lives, blessing our relationships with each other and with the world and with our own selves. Religion is always imperfect because it is full of imperfect people, but there's a security inherent in a tradition that is thousands of years old. It's worth cultivating a sort of sober hope in religion, because, as the Hierophant shows us, religion offers us a great gift. It gives us a way to interpret mysteries, to give weight and meaning to our lives. It gives a structure in which to recognize and respond to God's call, and it helps us work with each other to allow that call to change us. This is what the Hierophant shows us—that religion can provide a framework for holding the deep tension between earthly certainty and divine mystery, and a communion of people who wrestle with that same tension.

REFLECTIONS

- Reflect on the moments in your life that have felt charged with meaning. Do you feel like your religious tradition helps you to honor those moments? Why or why not?
- The Hierophant represents the structure of organized religion. What is your relationship with religion like? Do you feel comfortable within that structure? Why or why not?

- Reflect on the verses from Ephesians that tell us that, within the structure of Christianity, we are "no longer strangers and aliens" but "citizens with the saints." Do you feel like that sense of community plays a part in your spiritual life? Or does your spiritual life feel more solitary? Why?
- Are there prayers you recite when you feel like you don't have the right words to express your feelings? What is it about these prayers that draws you to them?
- The Hierophant is a revealer of mysteries. Do you feel like religion reveals mysteries for you? Why or why not?
- Reflect on the idea that you are a part of the "dwelling place for God." How does that change your perception of yourself and your life?

THE LOVERS

I give you a new commandment, that you love one another. Just as I have loved you, you also should love one another. (John 13:34)

We are creatures of relationship; the vocation to companionship is written into our very natures. The Lovers speaks to this bone-deep instinct to be in connection with other people, recognizing both the divinity of the desire for union and the fact that God is always present in our relationships with each other. Traditionally, the imagery of this card borrows heavily from the biblical story of Adam and Eve. In this story, Adam remains an incomplete being until the creation of Eve. He is not a full person until he is able to be in relationship with another. This story, and tarot's Lovers, is a reminder that, in Christianity, there is no "I" without "thou."

There can be no personal self that is not related to another self. Our task, as depicted in the Lovers, is to accept this gift of relationship and to delight in God by delighting in the fact of each other, with every person we meet.

In the Lovers, the couple stand naked before each other. Like Adam and Eve before the Fall, they see each other fully and without shame. One of the greatest gifts of love is this feeling of being truly perceived by another person. To see another person in the full measure of their reality—this is what it means to delight in someone. This kind of gaze is a particular gift from God. In the story of Adam and Eve, when God says, "It is not good that the man should be alone" (Genesis 2:18), what God means is that it is not good that a person should love no one but themselves. We are called by God to turn our gaze to others and to remember that other people are just as real and deserving of love as we ourselves are. When we do this, we honor the rich mysteriousness of them. We open ourselves to all their complications, their true and messy selves. We see them in their spiritual nakedness and are given the blessed opportunity to say, "Yes, you are good."

In the Waite-Smith depiction of the Lovers, we see an angel performing a benediction, blessing the connection between the lovers themselves. This is a reminder of what happens when we open ourselves up to the kind of relationship in which we are committed to the full reality of a person. We start to see the person as God sees them, and God sees us all with excruciating tenderness. To love another person in this way is to consciously, constantly be reminded that the other person is beloved and should be treated accordingly. This kind of love requires great courage because it requires leaving the ease and comfort of the self in order to step fully into a love that is closer to divine. But it's worth being courageous, because there's no greater way to love a person.

This kind of Christian love changes our relationships, because at its best, it spills out of our partnerships and into all of our interactions with others. It is easier to love the people we like in this intimate, naked way. But what is so radical about the Christian faith is that it calls us to love in this way every single person we meet. It's a commandment from God to love one another as God has loved us, and God is no mean lover. The idea of loving people in this way can seem overwhelming, but it also has the ability to transform our lives into a source of rich, ongoing joy. Love like this is not a singular and static choice. Love like this is not something we decide to do one time in order to check Christian charity off our to-do list. It is a conscious choice to find the miracle of God in every face, in every interaction, in every person we like and every person we don't. It is an impossible, mythical standard of love, and yet we are called to it all the same.

REFLECTIONS

- Do you have an easy time opening yourself up to love in the vulnerable way we see in tarot's Lovers? Why or why not?
- What are some ways in which you can extend Christian love to the people in your life, especially the people in your life you don't find naturally lovable?
- How do you like being loved? What makes you feel truly seen?
- In what ways do you enjoy loving others? How can you share your particular gifts of love with other people?
- Reflect on the idea that God is present in all our relationships. How does that make you feel?

- The kind of love Christianity calls us to is a naked outpouring of love toward every person we meet, to love our neighbor as an extension of ourselves. How does it feel for you to be held to a nearly impossible standard of love? Does it feel like a cruelty? Or like the best kind of challenge? Why?

THE CHARIOT

Beware of practicing your piety before others in order to be seen by them; for then you have no reward from your Father in heaven. (Matthew 6:1)

The Chariot is a classic depiction of golden, triumphant victory. It calls to mind Helios pulling the sun across the skies each day, Automedon steering Achilles into battle on the fields outside of Troy, Roman military processions making their way to the Campidoglio to receive scepters and laurel wreaths. It reminds us of the sheer strength of the human will. This is what people are capable of, with discipline and virtue. The tarot's charioteer achieves greatness through grit and determination and focus, but he does not do so on his own. Our will is a gift from God, but unfettered, it can lead to an excess of pride. This is the slippery, secret danger of glory, the way we so easily twist our impulses toward goodness to satisfy our own need for praise, our own desire to be the hero. If we look closely, the Chariot shows us how to remain humble in the cultivation of virtue, how to hold glory lightly and with a steady hand.

If all we offer the Chariot is one quick glance, all we see is that traditional depiction of glory. We see a man alone, a sole victor, a reminder of the danger of centering the self in our quest for virtue. Our desire to do good things, even great things, can give us a temptation to glory that pulls us into ourselves. This is an easy thing to do, letting the ego take over in our pursuit of virtue, because we want to be victorious through our own measures. It is natural to want to act in our own names, to be the master instead of the servant, to move the world instead of allowing ourselves to be moved by God. When we center ourselves in our goodness, though, it creates in us a sort of hero complex. The Chariot reminds us that victory achieved in seeming solitude can be quite dangerous, leading to a festering self-centeredness and a deifying of the self.

We are not God. We are not the saviors of the world. We are the servants, and if we look more closely and move past the golden flatness of the Chariot's victory, this is the deeper meaning we find. Our charioteer isn't holding any reins. He's not the one steering his chariot. He is allowing himself to be led by something else, something much greater than himself. God has given us free will, but we are also, somewhat counterintuitively, called to place our will in service to God. As God is ultimately unknowable to us, this can feel incredibly difficult. The carriage in the tarot's Chariot is drawn by two sphinxes, symbols of mystery. We are called to be led this way, too, by mysterious and enigmatic forces beyond our comprehension. We are called to surrender our will to the mysteriousness of the will of God, to seek goodness not in the shimmering victory of the world but in the kind of quiet virtue that may not earn us praise, in a servitude that we may not ever fully understand.

To do this—to live in service to God's will and God's victory—requires a constant cultivation of humility. Humility chafes against much of what we instinctively feel about what it means to be a good person. To decenter ourselves in our search for goodness seems against our natures. We want to do good things, and we want others to notice the good things we do, and we want praise for doing those good things. This is a natural human impulse, but we have to learn how to balance our desire for good with our need to remember that everything we do should point to God and not to us. The tarot's charioteer understands this. Standing under a canopy that separates him from heaven, he does not associate himself with God, because he is conscious of the difference. He holds in himself the knowledge that he is below God in all things. This is what the Chariot teaches us: it is possible to be heroic without centering our heroism, to cultivate virtue without demanding praise for virtue, and to seek good without making an idol of our goodness.

REFLECTIONS

- What images and stories do you associate with victory? Why?
- The Chariot speaks to us of the dangers of the unchecked will. Have you ever let your will override your sense of virtue? If so, how did you correct it?
- What are some ways in which you can cultivate the charioteer's humility in your own life?

- Do you feel comfortable doing good deeds in secret? Or do you feel let down when you aren't praised for your goodness? What might the answers to those questions have to teach you about your relationship with virtue?

- Reflect on the idea that we are called to let God be in control of our lives, even (maybe especially) when God's motives feel mysterious to us. Does it feel like a relief, or does it feel scary? Why?

- What is the difference between goodness and glory? If they feel the same to you, how can you separate them in your mind?

STRENGTH

Blessed are the meek, for they will inherit the earth.
(Matthew 5:5)

Saint Francis de Sales once said, "Nothing is so strong as gentleness, nothing so gentle as real strength." These words can seem radically counterintuitive to the way we often think about strength. Secular culture, particularly in the West, tends to associate strength with power and force, with independence and individualism. Both the Christian tradition and the tarot give us something different—a strength born not of power, but of weakness. In the Waite-Smith depiction of this virtue, the lion is as gentle as a lamb, and he has been tamed not by force, but by love. This is a strength that is merciful and tender and kind. This kind of strength can appear powerless, but true power always does, as it overcomes every obstacle in its own gentle way. It turns the other cheek and, in doing so, changes the enemy into the friend. It's the kind of strength that comes straight from the heart and turns the world on its head.

This gentle strength is the particular scandal of Christianity. The central tenet of our faith is that God became man to save us, but God became man in the most astonishing way. He did not come as a warrior. He did not come as a king. He did not come into the world in shining and spectacular power, as he certainly could have done. God came into the world as a nobody from the dusty backwater town of Nazareth, and he spent his life saving us not with force but with the gentlest of healing touches. His power lay in giving his power away, in refusing to use it on us and instead treating us with the greatest tenderness. There was immense strength in Jesus's life on earth, but it was a humble and wholly unexpected sort of strength, and it's one we see in the tarot as well. This is what the Waite-Smith depiction of Strength shows us, a meek woman taming brutal animality not with physical force or dazzling power but with soft hands, with the shock of powerlessness. What this archetype shows us is that strength is not found in conquering but in caretaking. Strength is not self-assertion, but self-abnegation.

This sort of meekness can seem beyond us, but we are called to cultivate it all the same. It can be terrifying to lean into this paradoxical kind of strength, because it is so at odds with how the world tells us to be. It will make us appear weak to the eyes of the world. It will make us appear soft and foolish. To love our enemies, to turn the other cheek, will make us seem as strange to the world now as Jesus seemed to the world two thousand years ago. To relinquish any worldly strength is extravagantly naive, and we must do it anyway. If we will be blessed, we must give up any power we hold, over and over again. We must be like the woman in the Strength card, stroking the lion with the softest touch and no defense, because nothing is so strong as gentleness and nothing brings cruelty to its knees like wholly unexpected vulnerability.

Jesus tells us that if we do this, we will be blessed, but we cannot access this kind of strength on our own. Human instinct insists that we hold on to every scrap of power we can muster in an effort to protect ourselves, and we are hard-pressed to give it up on our own. In the Waite-Smith depiction of Strength, the woman has a lemniscate above her head. This symbol of eternity suggests an innate connection with the eternal rhythm of God's time. The lemniscate reminds us that we can only cultivate this gentle strength by being so close to the heart of God that we can hear its beating. Our strength must be the strength not of our own selves but of immense faith. In this way, we create a perfect harmony between the divine will and the human response, and we are able to tame the lion with love instead of hate. "Blessed are the meek," indeed.

REFLECTIONS

- What images and ideas come to mind when you reflect on the idea of strength?
- What practices in your life help you react to situations with gentleness instead of anger, as the woman tames the lion?
- Have you ever experienced a moment when you expected someone to react with force and they instead reacted with gentleness? If so, what was that experience like for you?
- The Strength card reminds us that remaining close to the heart of God can help us to cultivate gentleness. Do

you see that idea played out in your own faith life? If so, how?

- Do you feel comfortable with the idea of intentionally pursuing meekness? Why or why not?
- How can you love your enemies today? How can you maintain the gentle spirit of tarot's Strength card?

THE HERMIT

Now during those days he went out to the mountain
to pray; and he spent the night in prayer to God.
(Luke 6:12)

The desert fathers and mothers were early Christians who fled into
the desert to find God. These men and women felt that it was
dangerous to passively accept the values of their society, and they
dealt with this temptation by removing themselves from it, escaping to the wilderness to live in a different way. The tarot's Hermit
is reminiscent of these men and women of the desert. He has severed himself from the noisy, greedy chaos of the world in order to
live in solitude, to confront himself and to find God. In letting
go of worldly distractions, he has made room for deeper spiritual

wisdom, and he uses that wisdom to light the way for others. The Hermit leads us into his silent, solitary desert and teaches us how to live from that place.

The Hermit is defined by his solitude; the word "hermit" comes from the Greek *erēmos,* meaning "desolate." In our modern world, we tend to think of solitude in terms of self-care, a way to retreat from daily life in order to rest and refresh ourselves. The Hermit's solitude is something altogether different and more extreme. It is not the solitude of rest but the solitude of conversion. It is not the solitude of refreshment but the solitude of death. Like the desert fathers, the tarot's Hermit has retreated from the world in order to strip himself to nothingness, and he has succeeded. Standing on a stark and snowy ground in front of a gray sky, he almost recedes into the background. Here is a self that is wholly unburdened by the attachments and expectations of the world. Here is a self that is free to encounter the living God.

Through tarot's history, the Hermit has often been associated with the virtue of prudence. One of the four cardinal virtues, prudence is the ability to judge wisely the best course of action in one's life. Though it has become increasingly associated with the idea of cautiousness, it is about much more than simply refusing to take risks. It is about knowing oneself and one's path clearly so as to be able to discern caution versus cowardice, mercy versus weakness, intelligence versus cunning, what is truly right versus what is almost right. We see this virtue played out in the imagery of the Hermit. He is alone, but he is not a wanderer. Head down, staff in hand, he treads his path ever so carefully. This sagacity— this prudence—is the result of the Hermit's solitude. This spiritual wisdom is the gift that solitude gives. In stripping away the false self, the Hermit has made room for true spiritual wisdom. The path of virtue becomes clear for prudent footsteps.

It might be easy to label the Hermit as a misanthrope, a man too focused on his own interior journey to care about anyone else. After all, here is a man who has left the whole world behind. But while the Hermit may be solitary, he is not unloving. While he may have a vested interest in his own interior life, he has a vested interest in ours as well. His wisdom is not his alone, but his to share, and share it he will. He is a sage, not simply searching for spiritual truth but bringing it to others. Carrying a lamp, he lights his own path and lights a way for us. Like the desert fathers, he carries hard-won wisdom. And if we listen, we, too, can follow the Hermit's path, can humble ourselves and turn ourselves into the kind of people who can live in the same place of interior stillness. When we have lost ourselves in solitude and found ourselves in God, we can carry our own bright lamps of wisdom, guiding others to the gift of solitude and prudence.

REFLECTIONS

- Do you find it comfortable to be truly alone with yourself? Why or why not?
- What aspects of your life keep you from the solitude and silence of the Hermit? Can you change them? How?
- Is there someone in your life who has been for you like the tarot's Hermit, lighting your way with spiritual wisdom? If so, how have they changed your path?
- Have you experienced the solitude of the Hermit in your own life? If so, how did it change you?

- Reflect on the virtue of prudence. Do you feel like that's an accessible virtue for you? How can you cultivate prudence in your own life?
- Do you feel as if you have a lamp to carry as the Hermit does? What spiritual light have you found in yourself that you can bring to others?

WHEEL OF FORTUNE

The human mind plans the way, but the Lord directs the steps. (Proverbs 16:9)

Our lives are never static. We live in a constant dance between joy and sorrow, hibernation and exploration, satisfaction and desire. The Wheel of Fortune is a reminder of this perpetual change, the ever-turning wheel of our lives. It also speaks to how often these changes feel largely out of our control. Traditionally, the Wheel of Fortune symbolizes the idea of fate. We turn and turn on the wheel of life, and it often seems as if things just happen to us. We are subject to the alternation of chance, which is itself subject to the dominion of a fate wholly unknown to us. These strange animals that closely surround the wheel—a sphinx, a snake, a dog-headed man reminiscent of the Egyptian god Anubis—are symbols of the mysteriousness of the wheel. They are a reminder that there is so very much that is beyond our control or understanding. In this way, the Wheel of Fortune can feel like a sort of cosmic shrug. We are born, we live good lives and bad lives, and then we die. Life is just riding it out.

The Wheel of Fortune speaks to this feeling, to the way our lives can feel subject to chance and only as big as we are. To feel this way, like we have no choice but to ride the waves of good luck and bad luck, is a bleak way to live. There is more, though, and the Waite-Smith Wheel of Fortune points us to it and pulls us out of the cursed meaninglessness of fate. Outside of the Wheel of Fortune, at the four corners of the image, we see the traditional symbols of the authors of the four Gospels: the angel for Matthew, the winged lion for Mark, the winged ox for Luke, and the eagle for John. They frame our wheel not with fate but with the life of Christ, giving us a vast and miraculous new perspective. God became man and dwelt among us, and it is not an exaggeration to say that this changed everything. The Incarnation is the greatest miracle of Christianity, and to live as a Christian is to live in a world pierced and wholly infused by this miracle. We are indeed subject to lives over which we often have little control, but they are not lives ruled by the cruel touch of fate. Framed by the Incarnation and by the life of Christ, our lives are moved not by chance but by the love of God. We, as Christians, get to believe in something more than fate. More than that, we have a responsibility to believe in something more than fate. We are not allowed nihilism. We are not allowed the cosmic shrug. We are given something more: a chance to know that God loves us too much to turn us over to fate, a chance to grab the freely given gift of salvation.

This is a gift, to know that our lives are touched by love and are therefore more meaningful than a roll of the dice, but it doesn't always make our lives feel more comfortable. Our lives are moved by the love of God, but whether we live in the hands of fate or in the hands of God, it can still feel out of our control. God may be more loving, but God is not more known. Even when viewed in the light of Christian faith, the Wheel of Fortune promises change, but it never promises comfort. To live in that change, as we all do, unable to see what's around the next curve of the wheel, is genuinely difficult sometimes. But we are lucky, because it is much easier to do this when we remember that God holds all of us in the palm of his hand, that we turn on a wheel that is in the control of our God. Both of these things are true—that God loves us and also that our lives often seem subject to chance because God is ultimately unknowable to us. This is the task of faith, to hold both of these beliefs lightly, to dance between and around the two.

REFLECTIONS

- Do you feel as if God has a specific hand in your life? Or do you believe in a less personally involved God? Why?
- Do you ever feel anxious about all the uncontrollable variables of life, all the turns of the wheel? If so, does it bring you peace to think of your life being in God's hands? Why or why not?
- Reflect on the idea that your life has meaning because you are made by God and that God cares for you. How would living with that idea in mind change the course of your life?
- Do you feel like the life of Christ frames your own life as it does in this image? Why or why not?

- Do you believe in miracles? In God's ability to change the turn of the wheel? If not, what might it feel like to believe that miracles are possible?
- Do you feel as if you let God have control of your life? Or do you yourself try to keep control of your own fate? What might it feel like to loosen your own grasp on your life?

JUSTICE

The Spirit of the Lord is upon me, because he has anointed me to bring good news to the poor. He has sent me to proclaim release to the captives and recovery of sight to the blind, to let the oppressed go free. (Luke 4:18)

The idea of justice often calls to mind the righting of wrongs and the punishment of people who do bad things. Holding scales for the weighing of evidence and a sword with which she wields her authority, the traditional figure of Justice depicted in the Waite-Smith deck does speak to this popular view. Justice as a Christian virtue, however, is something different and deeper. In the Gospels, Jesus tells his disciples that the greatest commandment is to love God and to love our neighbor. For Christians, this is justice. For

Christians, justice is the virtue that teaches us how to love our neighbor well. A Christian who lives justly is always looking for ways to give their due to God and neighbor. We practice justice when we live from the belief that all human beings are beloved children of God, worthy of rights and dignity. Seen in this way, Lady Justice's scales are for lifting the poor, and her sword is for casting down the mighty, and justice becomes less about how efficiently we can punish and more about how well we can love.

To be just is to love our neighbor, and the Bible is very clear that our neighbors are the poor and the vulnerable. The Old Testament speaks of God as being "Father of orphans and protector of widows" (Psalm 68:5). The God of the Old Testament identifies with the powerless and takes up their cause, and the laws of ancient Israel reflected this in the many specific ways they tasked the Israelites with caring for the most vulnerable among them, from leaving grain in the fields for the poor to forgiving debts every seven years. This care for the poor flows seamlessly into the New Testament. God identifies so deeply with the outcast that he himself became an outcast. Jesus was born in a stable and spent his whole life among the vulnerable. From the Sermon on the Mount to the parable of the Good Samaritan, Jesus spent his entire ministry teaching us how to love the people who most need love. Over and over again, we see God exercise his power for the empowerment of the poor. God takes up their cause, and the virtue of justice calls us to this as well.

If being just is about giving our due to God and neighbor, it follows that justice is a thing lived out in our relationships day by day. Practicing justice requires constant, sustained reflection and circumspection, but it is a virtue practiced only in connection with other people. In this way, Christian justice is inevitably social justice; it compels us to change our own lives in order to change the lives of others. Justice is a proactive virtue, one that calls us to become deeply involved in the lives of the poor and vulnerable, working to make their lives not only bearable but delightful and full of joy. To treat each person we meet with justice is to love them as much as we love ourselves, which means more than fulfilling their basic needs. To live justly is to live in actual, loving relationship with them, to give them as much as we give ourselves. We cannot truly practice justice while keeping ourselves above anyone else.

Behind tarot's figure of Justice hangs a purple veil, the color which, in the Christian life, represents penance and sacrifice. The paradox of Christian justice is that we do not enact sacrifices for others but take on the sacrifices ourselves. Christian justice is not about vengeance and it is not about judgment. It is not about meting out punishment for others and it is not about avoiding punishment for ourselves. It is about actively working to care for our neighbors, no more and no less. To love people in this way—to seek justice in this way—humbles us. To lift up the vulnerable as God calls us to do nearly always requires lowering ourselves, and so purification of the heart and love for the poor are of a piece. Living justly frees us to live in love, giving others their due without appointing ourselves the judges of others' lives. This kind of justice, when lived well, is virtue not of retribution but of generosity in all things.

REFLECTIONS

- Do you think of justice as primarily private or social? Why?
- Do you think of justice as a virtue of connection or of detachment? Why?

- What ideas come up for you when you reflect on the idea of justice? Are they rooted more in love or in punishment? Why?
- Who are your neighbors? How can you care for them today?
- Christian justice—loving our neighbors as ourselves—necessitates a change in how one lives. What are some small and tangible ways you can change your life in order to better practice the virtue of justice?
- Reflect on your ideas of Christian justice. For you, do Christianity and justice feel opposed? Or intertwined? In what ways?

THE HANGED MAN

Do not be conformed to this world, but be transformed by the renewing of your minds, so that you may discern what is the will of God—what is good and acceptable and perfect. (Romans 12:2)

We live between the two gravitational fields of heaven and earth, both of them always trying to pull us closer. God wants us, but the world wants us, too, and in every moment of our lives we have a choice to let ourselves be pulled one way or the other. The Hanged Man is a symbol of what it feels like to gravitate more toward heaven than toward earth. He is flipped upside down because he has surrendered himself to God. He can no longer resist the appeal from above, the call to live for something different than what the world offers. This is what it is like to live as a child of heaven, to be shaped by God, to live in the world but not of it.

All the time, in little ways and big ways, the world prompts us to live for our own gain. But heaven tells us to live for God, and this is what the Hanged Man does. He lives upside down because he moves his feet to the rhythm of heaven instead of earth. The "solid ground" under his feet is found above, and the ground below is not the concern of his soul. He has placed God's will above his own will and is pulled to virtue as a result. The Hanged Man speaks to the way in which doing this—following God in all things—can feel like an act of suspension. In committing to something outside of himself, he has flipped himself into a pose of true vulnerability. This is what it feels like to trust in God instead of in our own selves. This is what it feels like to place our faith in a force we can't ever fully know. It can be deeply uncomfortable, but the Hanged Man shows us how to suspend ourselves in this perpetual posture of humility, permanently shifting our center of gravity from ourselves to God. He offers us an example of how to live in this liminal space, letting heaven guide us even while we move in the world.

In the Gospel of Matthew, Jesus tells his disciples that they cannot serve God and money, that no man can serve two masters. The Hanged Man has a true understanding of this teaching to abandon worldly power and to choose God instead. In early tarot decks, the Hanged Man was often called the Traitor, because this is how traitors were punished in fifteenth-century Italy, hung upside down by one foot. This original meaning of treachery and betrayal is still relevant. In order to live as the Hanged Man does, we have to become, in some sense, traitors to a world that promises us that money and power and pride will make us happy. The Hanged Man knows better. To live as he does is to follow the example of Jesus tempted in the desert, rejecting all the empty promises of worldly power and prestige. It is to seek humility instead of pride, faith instead of egoism, service to others instead of power over them. It is to make a conscious choice to serve a different master, because we cannot serve both.

There is a tension in living this way. To live as the Hanged Man instructs us to live is to remember, constantly, that we live *in* the world but that we are not *of* the world. It is to live always in a sharp moment of being neither here nor there, neither one thing nor another. It is a life suspended, crucified between heaven and earth, always a little out of place. This tension is an ever-present reminder that we belong to heaven, to the place where we are not yet. It can feel paradoxical, like loneliness and belonging in the same breath. But we are not alone in the world so much as we are living in constant reminder that we are children of heaven. In this way, the Hanged Man, crowned with a bright halo, shows us that we are born for something else, and he gently pushes us to allow ourselves to be transformed by this, to bear witness to Christ and not to the world, to seek goodness in the world while living suspended in wait for heaven.

REFLECTIONS

- In what specific ways do you feel as if the world tries to pull you to itself and away from heaven?
- In your own life, do you feel the tension seen in the Hanged Man, suspended between the gravitational poles of earth and heaven? If so, what does that feel like?
- What would it take for you to place God's will above your own will, to metaphorically flip yourself as the Hanged Man does?

- Romans 12:2 calls us to be "transformed by the renewing of [our] minds," so that we can know God's will. How can you change your patterns of thought in order to gain the Hanged Man's saintly halo?
- In your life, do you seek to glorify yourself or to glorify God? Where does your center of gravity lie? Why?
- Do you ever feel lonely or out of place in your pursuit of the Christian life? How does it feel to seek heaven while living in the world?

DEATH

Where, O death, is your victory? Where, O death, is your sting? (1 Corinthians 15:55)

Death is the most commonplace of happenings, the one thing that comes for us all. We know this, but we fight it all the same. We create endless diversions to distract ourselves from death. We praise youthfulness as some sort of virtue, always grasping to be eternally ageless. We think of death as the ultimate defeat, the end of all our attempts to control our lives. And still, we die. Tarot's Death card, at its simplest, helps us to face these fears of death. It is a sort of *memento mori,* a way of keeping close to our hearts the unpredictable end of life and letting it change how we live today. The practice of *memento mori*—Latin for "remember your death"—can seem macabre or depressing for those of us who are always trying to shuffle death off the stage. For Christians, though, it is a hopeful practice. This life is not all there is. We are made for more, and we get to face death with courage.

One of the greatest gifts of Christianity is the knowledge that death is not the end. We believe in the resurrection of Jesus Christ, and this belief has the ability to fundamentally change our relationship with death. Jesus died a real bodily death. The Son of God himself suffered the same death that we will all suffer, the same death that is a part of the human condition. In doing so, he participated in the death of every one of us. Jesus died the death of all, and then he rose from the dead, body and soul, never to die again. Jesus showed us that there is a love that is stronger even than death, that God loves us with a love so mighty it can conquer the one thing we can never conquer on our own. In doing so, Jesus transformed the curse of death into a blessing and gave us a resurrection on which to stake our lives.

When we believe in the resurrection, we trade fear for hope, and this hope shapes our entire Christian lives, from birth to death. In the Waite-Smith Death card, there is a river that runs in the background, reminding us that death is connected with the sacrament of baptism. When we are baptized, we participate sacramentally in the death of Christ; we die to a life of sin and are reborn into a life of grace. There is living water in us, water that murmurs and calls us to God. For Christians, physical death is not the end of life but simply the final calling, a completion of the "dying with Christ" that happens in baptism. It is an act of entering the life to which we are called. This is what is essentially different about the Christian view of death. It is not the ultimate evil or the great unknown; it is, as tarot shows us, the path to the rising sun, the doorway to spending eternity with God. We know that death is not the end but a beginning, and so we are able, like the priest in tarot's Death card, to greet death as a friend.

In the Death card, everyone is confronted by death: king, priest, woman, child. It comes for us all, we know not when. We cannot escape it, and so the only thing we can change is how we meet it. If we live in the love of Christ, there is grace and strength for the moment when we pass from this life to the next. If we truly believe that God came into our world and conquered death itself, then death is not something we should fear. In this way, how we deal with death is a form of witness. We know that we will all meet death eventually, but we also know that we can meet death with peace and courage. Reflecting on our deaths should not scare us but help us realize that our time on this earth is limited and what we do now echoes in eternity. We must learn to embrace our mortality because it is the thing that defines us as human beings—fallen and fallible, but immensely loved—and made for more.

REFLECTIONS

- Do you feel comfortable thinking about death? Or is it something you instinctively shy away from? Why?
- Reflect on the idea that, as Christians, our deaths provide a way to witness to others. How might that change your perspective on your own future death?
- Spend some time with each of the four people in tarot's Death card. What are their different reactions to death?
- Tarot's death card can be seen as a *memento mori*. What are some other *memento mori* practices you can bring into your life?

- Reflect on Romans 6:3—"Do you not know that all of us who have been baptized into Christ Jesus were baptized into his death?" Do you see baptism as a participation in Christ's death? In light of this verse, how might your own eventual death be seen as a completion of your baptism?
- Do you feel like your faith helps you to face death with courage? Why or why not?

TEMPERANCE

Above all, clothe yourselves with love, which binds everything together in perfect harmony.
(Colossians 3:14)

We all have in us the risen Christ and Adam's fall. We are all both children of heaven and children of earth, a bittersweet blessing. The bittersweetness comes from the tension: while we want to live for heaven, we also want to live for *here* and *now*. Temperance is the virtue that keeps us in good balance as we do this. Temperance encourages us to love ourselves enough to create the boundaries we need to live well. It is, at its simplest, a selfless turning to the self. It holds us in the gentler flow of life and keeps us close to God. As the Waite-Smith image shows us, it is the angel on the shore, one foot in water and one on land, who stands before the blessed path to the rising sun. When following the example of this angel in living truly temperate lives, we are able to realize what is actually good, rather than whatever simply feels good in any given moment, and as a result, we are able to move toward lives that are truly fulfilling for us. Temperance shows us how to hold the various parts of ourselves in balance, creating an easy flow that allows us to know and love ourselves with good intention.

Other virtues teach us how to relate to other people, but temperance is exceptional in that it specifically teaches us how to relate to ourselves. We tend to associate temperance with self-control, but it is more than that: temperance is about self-control, but it's also about self-love. Temperance teaches us how to examine ourselves in gentleness without becoming myopically fixed on ourselves, how to uplift our natural inclination to enjoy life without descending into selfishness, how to love ourselves with grace and understanding. In doing this, temperance, like all virtues, turns us to God. If we practice temperance as Christianity teaches it, eventually we see into ourselves deeply enough to recognize that we are children of God. We are, each of us, made with care by a loving Creator, and we deserve to love ourselves as God loves us, to give ourselves and our lives as much care as God gives them. It matters how we live.

Temperance is a self-centered virtue—this angel is fixed on her own tempered cup—but it is not selfish. It is good to give true attention to our souls, and in teaching us to examine ourselves with love, temperance has an uncanny ability to keep us truly humble. When we are focused on ordering our own souls, we are less focused on judging the souls of others. This is a good thing, not least because temperance is a deeply personal virtue, one that flows differently for every person. There are no hard-and-fast, universal rules about what temperance should look like. We all vary in our attitudes toward ourselves and our passions, and so we all have our own particular tendencies to flood the banks of moderation and order in our own lives. Like tarot's angel of Temperance, we have permission to keep our eyes on our own cups.

Modern culture likes to associate temperance with repression of desire, but temperance is not about removing all pleasure from one's life. Temperance's angel stands on a beautiful shore, accompanied by blooming flowers and a fresh new dawn. There is true pleasure here! To be mistrustful of all passion is to live a mealy and soft theology. The true goal of temperance is not loss of feeling or toothless tranquility. It is blessedness. We all have a natural will to live, to enjoy life, and temperance does not work against this. Temperance asks us to hold our passions accountable; it does not ask us to erase them. Real temperance is full of ease and joy and an inclination toward true happiness. It is moderation, but moderation swings both ways. It is self-control, but it is so much more, too.

REFLECTIONS

- Reflect on your ideas about the virtue of temperance. What images and ideas and feelings does it bring up for you?
- Do you ever think about your desires in the context of whether or not they bring you closer to God? How might that change your relationship with desire?
- Spend some time honestly meditating on the state of your life. Do you feel as if it has an easy, balanced flow, like we see in tarot's Temperance card? Are there parts of it that don't flow well, desires that are either dammed up or rushing frantically?

- Do you ever feel in yourself an urge to judge others' apparent temperance or lack thereof? If so, how can you train yourself to keep your eyes on your own soul as Temperance's angel does?
- What does a temperate life look like for you?
- What parts of your life steer you toward intemperance? How can you change those aspects of your life to flow more gently?

THE DEVIL

But one is tempted by one's own desire, being lured and enticed by it. (James 1:14)

Within each virtue is the seed of vice. We have an instinct to seek goodness and truth and beauty, but none of us are perfect, and we also have an instinct to take things too far. We want to *be* good, but we also want to *feel* good, and so temperance slips into gluttony, love into lust, humility into envy. The Devil holds up a mirror to this instinct, showing us what happens when we take pleasure too far. In the Devil, we see the kind of hedonism that is enjoying oneself to the detriment of others, enriching oneself at the expense of others, taking chances on the backs of others. It's what happens when we put our own pleasure above the good of all. It is sin as the pursuit of personal gain and power with no regard to the lives of our fellow human beings. The Devil shows us what happens when we let our egos override our charity and when we let that small seed of vice grow, and what a lonely life that is.

The Devil is not so much about the metaphysics of evil as it is about the ways in which we voluntarily forfeit our freedom to selfish desire. It is no accident that the two figures in this card are in chains. They are not the children of this Devil but its parents. They have created this monster and are now beholden to it, unable to escape. This centering of the self above all else creates a sort of spiritual imprisonment. It introduces a certain claustrophobic hollowness into our existence, chaining us to our own wants at the expense of anything else. This kind of hedonistic pleasure reduces us to a state of passivity, trapping us in an endless cycle of feeding an immoderate desire, no matter the cost. In this way, the inner heart of sin is not so much the presence of evil as it is the absence of love. It is an empty, negative force in our lives. To live with tarot's Devil is to be trapped by a thing visible only by the suffering it causes.

There is a deep loneliness in living this way. It separates us from each other, because when we live only for our own pleasure, we cannot live for each other. As Christians, our connections with other people draw us closer to God, and so wherever there is alienation from other people, there is inevitably alienation from God. When we make a habit of centering our own selves in our lives, we eventually lose the ability to be in vulnerable connection with other people. When we treat other people only as objects for our own gain, we sever our connection with them. We cannot see them as fellow children of God. Sin is, at its root, a failure to love anything outside of oneself, defined not so much by turning toward something but by turning away from each other. It is virtue twisted monstrously in on itself for its own gain. Because of this, the Devil is tarot's Lovers in reverse. It is an ultimately isolating figure, tearing us away from the ability to truly love each other.

The Devil can be a difficult image for some. That being said, if we believe in God's love, then we must also recognize the forces that work against that love. Ultimately, this is all the tarot's Devil asks us to do. There is good in confronting our own weaknesses, in looking for the fault lines in our souls, in taking an honest look at ourselves, and tarot's Devil encourages us to do just that. It can be disheartening, to say the least, to think about the ways in which we are apt to fail each other and God. But our weaknesses never prevent God's goodness from working, so we can hold the Devil lightly. The Devil is a reminder that to live only for oneself is to live in hell, but God is always looking to connect with us in gentleness and love, to free us from these bonds we make for ourselves.

REFLECTIONS

- Are there any parts of your life in which you feel inclined toward selfishness? If so, how can you correct them?
- Tarot's Devil shows us sin as a sort of imprisonment. Reflect on the idea of sin as imprisonment and virtue as freedom. Might that change how you feel about them? If so, in what ways?
- Reflect on your relationship with pleasure. Are there things in your life that you have trouble enjoying in a moderate way—things that feel like they control you rather than you controlling them? If so, how might you change your relationship with those things?
- The Devil can be a scary card inasmuch as it prompts us to reflect on our failures, but Isaiah 43:25 tells us that God "will not remember [our] sins." Are your failures something that you can hold as lightly as God

does? Or are you more apt to dwell on them? Why or why not?

- Have you ever let virtue slip into vice? How did it happen, and how did you change it?
- The Devil shows us the ultimately isolating effects of sin. How can you foster connection with other people as a way to pull outside of yourself and connect with God?

THE TOWER

O my God, I cry by day, but you do not answer; and by night, but find no rest. Yet you are holy, enthroned on the praises of Israel. In you our ancestors trusted; they trusted, and you delivered them. (Psalm 22:2–4)

It's easy to forget God when life is good. It's easy to feel like we are in control when problems are few. When things are going well, it's easy to make our lives our own business, magnanimously letting God play some bit part, maybe, but not the main role. We decide that we can handle things ourselves, that God is no longer necessary. We carefully craft our futures. We plan for pleasure and security. We make little gods of ourselves, building towers to put ourselves at the level of the Creator, all the while feeling pretty good about it. And then things fall apart. A serious illness. The death of a loved one. A financial catastrophe. Tragedy strikes, because suffering eventually comes for all of us. All the little towers we have so proudly built come tumbling down, and we realize that nothing is truly in our control. How we let that suffering change us—what we do with that pain—is the lesson of the Tower.

When we falsely convince ourselves that we are in control of our lives and then something terrible happens, anger at God is a natural response. When we make ourselves the center of our lives, every bad thing that happens to us feels like a personal attack. Any moment of suffering feels like a divine retribution bent on knocking down our pride. The lesson of the Tower, though, is not that all suffering is a punishment from God. Though the lightning bolt knocks the crown, no divine hand wields that power. We all suffer, eventually and to varying degrees. The impulse to blame God is natural, and God does not mind our anger, but neither does God wish for us to be in pain. We do not suffer because God hates us. We suffer because God has given us free will, and free will would cease to exist if God shielded us from every tragedy. What do we do with suffering, then? What do we do when life becomes too much for us to bear? What do we do in Tower moments?

The two people we see in the Tower are falling from a great height. In moments of great suffering, the ground opens up beneath us, the foundations of our lives shift, and our illusions of self-sufficiency are shattered. We are struck by the lightning bolt of a fact that anything can be taken from us at any moment, that all our grasps at control are worth nothing. It hurts to learn that, despite our best efforts, we do not control the universe. The Tower is an act of true humbling, and being humbled is painful. If we can move past the anger of wounded pride, though, we can let ourselves be cracked open by it. It is in this wound of humility that God comes in. Pain always insists upon being attended to in a way that comfort does not; God speaks to us in our pleasures, but God speaks to us in our pain as well.

The Tower is a difficult card, but it's also not a card that can be avoided forever. Suffering is a fact of human life; we cannot save ourselves from it, despite our best efforts. What's more, Christianity cannot save us from it, either. God promises us love, but God never promises us a life free from pain. What Christianity can do for us is make suffering more tolerable to bear. In Christianity, we have a God who sees our suffering. More than that, we have a God who loves us enough to bear our suffering alongside us. In Christ, God suffers with us, and suffering is easier to bear together than alone. The Tower knocks us down, but God is always present to catch us at the bottom of the fall, to pick us up and dust us off. God is always ready for us when we have nowhere else to turn, always ready to exalt those of us who are humble enough to ask for God's care, to recognize that nothing is truly in our control.

REFLECTIONS

- There are many passages in the Bible that speak to praising God even in suffering, including but not limited to Psalm 22:2–4, Job 1:21 ("The Lord gave, and the Lord has taken away; blessed be the name of the Lord.), and Habakkuk 3:17–18 ("Though the flock is cut off from the fold, and there is no herd in the stalls, yet I will rejoice in the Lord."). Spend some time with these verses. How does it feel to think about praising God even in Tower moments?
- Reflect on the idea of control, especially the ways in which our sense of control is questioned in the Tower.

Do you feel as if you are in control of your life? If so, do you feel as if your sense of control keeps you safe?

- Do you feel as if the suffering in your life is a punishment from God? Why or why not?

- Ultimately, tarot's Tower invites us into humility. The word "humble" comes from the Latin root *humus*, meaning "earth." How can you bring a clearer sense of groundedness or earthiness into your life?

- Are there parts of your life that you try to keep separate from God? How can you humbly offer those parts of your life to God?

- What would it feel like to let God have total control of your life? To lean on God in all things instead of build towers for yourself?

THE STAR

Let us hold fast to the confession of our hope without wavering, for he who has promised is faithful. (Hebrews 10:23)

Longing is in our nature. It is a fundamental part of who we are as human beings, this compulsion to tilt our heads up to the night sky and find something to wish on. We try to satisfy this instinctual longing in all sorts of ways: we chase money, authenticity, meaning, progress. We hope for small things—a new job, a new love, a new adventure—but when we receive them, it's never quite enough. Nothing here in this earthly life ever fully satisfies this compulsion of ours to reach for the stars. The Star speaks to this feeling that there is something more for which to reach. We have an aspiration for life—a longing for goodness—but God is the one who has placed it in our hearts, and God is the only one who can fulfill it. Only the infinite can open our hearts. Only God can satisfy the longing. This longing is a gift, and to come to know God is to receive the great hope that the Star proclaims, the hope that our longing will be fulfilled.

As Christians, we sometimes become so familiar with God that we almost cease to notice the possession of this hope, in the same way a busy person ceases to notice the stars in the night sky. We get lost in the bustle of day-to-day life, heads down, and forget to look up. God becomes just another part of the landscape of our lives. The wonder is always there, but it can go dormant. In many ways, the task of the tarot's Star is simply to pull us back to the wonder of God, to call us back to the gift of hope, to remind us that we are called to something outside of ourselves. We are made for love, and our lives have meaning beyond our wildest imaginings. We get to be loved by a God who is not just any god, but the God who loves each one of us with a specific and never-ending love. Not only that, but God has the ability and the desire to give us things we cannot give ourselves, and we get to hope for those things.

To believe in the goodness of God can feel like wishing on a shooting star—a sweet but ultimately meaningless ritual. Hope can feel childish, naive, and inaccessible. There is much suffering in the world, and sometimes it feels easier to sink into nihilism than to still believe that God broods over the world like a gentle mother hen, to still believe that there is goodness at the heart of things and not horror. This is why the hope of the Star is so radical. It is a belief in the transformability of things. Christians are called to believe in the possibility of love breaking into the dull sameness of the world. We are not called to a belief in coincidence but a belief in miracles. These little green shoots of goodness that we find in the world? They are not a careless shrug from an indifferent universe. They are a thing of God's love, watered as carefully as the woman in the Star waters the shore. Is it naive to believe this? Perhaps. Naivete is preferable to cynicism, though, and the more we water the ground of hope, the more goodness we see.

It requires great vulnerability to hope for goodness on such a grand scale. It is no coincidence that the woman in the Star is naked; she is a stark representation of how exposed it can make us feel to dare to believe that God plans something more for us. Hope is an exercise of desire, and this desire compels us to admit that the longing we feel is for something we cannot give ourselves. To hope is to admit, in the same breath, both that we have longing and that our longing deserves to be satisfied. For some of us, that can be deeply uncomfortable, but we cannot receive the hope of God if we never open ourselves up to the possibility of accepting it. The deep longing we feel will never be fulfilled if we do not allow it to be. The Star gently pushes us to unclothe our longing, expand our hearts, and dare to believe that we deserve all the goodness that God wants to give us.

REFLECTIONS

- What in your life helps you to cultivate the virtue of hope? How can you water those shoots of hope as the woman in the Star does?
- Reflect on the idea that hope requires vulnerability. Is it easy for you to be vulnerable in that way? Or do you feel more comfortable protecting your expectations? Why or why not?

- Is there anyone in your life whom you feel is a particularly hopeful person? What is it like to be around that person?
- Do you believe in miracles, in God's ability to give you as much as you can hope for? Why or why not?
- The Star teaches us that the more we water the ground of hope, the more stars of hope we see. Do you see hope in this way, as something that builds on itself? Why or why not?
- What do you hope for in this life? How can you allow yourself to hope for even more?

THE MOON

For as the heavens are higher than the earth, so are
my ways higher than your ways and my thoughts than
your thoughts. (Isaiah 55:9)

It is often easier to think about God than to love God. For many
of us, the realm of the mind is more comfortable than the realm of
the heart, and so we hold on to the facets of God that make sense
to us and push away the rest. Facts can only take us so far, though.
Strange and dreamlike, the Moon reminds us that to seek God
only through the mind does God a grave disservice. God cannot
be thought or constructed; God must be more than the object of
our reason. In seeking God, we will always eventually come up
against the limits of the mind. God is far beyond our understanding, and to admit this, as the Moon asks us to do, is to push past

those limits of the mind into the strange and dazzling darkness of unknowing. It is to cease the struggle to grasp God with the mind. It is to fully abandon the intellect for more intuitive means of knowing. It is to trust the sometimes uncomfortable darkness of God rather than try to understand it.

The first step of the Moon is a step of humility. It is to admit that, in this life, we see "in a mirror, dimly" (1 Corinthians 13:12). This is an uneasy step, as it reminds us of the limits of the reason to which we cling, but the Moon pushes us to acknowledge that, in truth, we know very little about God. In the Waite-Smith depiction of the Moon, the heavenly body is eclipsed. This is a true darkness. So much of God is hidden from us; there is so much that our intellects simply cannot grasp. We are creatures to the Creator, and our intellects are but a dark shadow compared to the true glory of God. God's thoughts are higher than our thoughts, and in our attempts to know God we are like animals howling at the moon. Our finite minds simply cannot comprehend the infinite. God is ultimately strange and mysterious to us, a thing unseeable and unsayable and unexplainable, a presence so far beyond our understanding that he can feel like a darkness to us.

The Moon can sometimes feel like an uncomfortable archetype, so dreamlike that it is difficult to grasp. It has a tendency to push the limits of our reason so far that we lose our center of intellectual gravity, but in doing so, the Moon gives us a gift. It re-invites us into faith. When we step into the humility of unknowing, we also step into trust. To believe in God is to have faith in the things we cannot understand. To stake our faith on only what we can grasp with our minds is no faith at all. The Moon reminds us that God does not operate according to our rules of logic, and therefore God does not have to interact with us according to those rules. We are below God in all things, including understanding, but if we can hold on to the light of faith and to this humble curiosity, it becomes an adventure to move quietly forward on the path into the dark landscape of the Moon, into all the things we do not know. God may feel hidden to us, but God is never apart from us. God is beyond our comprehension, but God is not beyond our faith.

If we can humble ourselves enough to acknowledge that we cannot know God fully, we learn that the mind is not the only path to God. We can come to God through knowing, but we can come to God through unknowing as well. Though we cannot understand God in this life, that does not mean we cannot still become what God wants us to be. The Moon invites us into a spiritual exercise of becoming rather than understanding, of moving into the unknowing rather than trying to think our way around it, of stepping fully into the bright darkness of God. Intelligence is a kind of knowing, but love is a kind of knowing, too, and in the dark night of the Moon, love leads the way. When it comes to God, there is little to learn with the mind, but there is everything to learn with the heart.

REFLECTIONS

- Do you feel as if you interact with God primarily through your intellect, or through other means? What might the answer to that question say about your personality and relationship with God?
- In tarot's Moon card there is a path that stretches to the very farthest horizon and beyond. The Moon can make us uneasy in its dreaminess, but is it perhaps possible to see the mysteriousness as an invitation into a journey?

- Reflect on the idea that you will never fully grasp God with your mind in this life. Does it change how you feel in relation to God? If so, in what ways?
- Do you feel comfortable simply being in God? Simply resting in the dark unknowing? Why or why not?
- In tarot's Moon, the moon is eclipsed and therefore unable to be seen, but it still contains a face. Do you feel like God can seem mysterious but also personal? Why or why not?
- Do you feel as if you have faith in the whole of God, or only in the parts of God you feel as if you understand? Why?

THE SUN

Again Jesus spoke to them, saying, "I am the light of the world. Whoever follows me will never walk in darkness but will have the light of life." (John 8:12)

To be a human is to love with the senses. We have souls, but we live in a physical world; we touch and taste and see, give with and of our bodies. This is how we love each other, and this is why it can be so difficult for us to love God. We long to see God's face, to love God as we are able to love each other. God, knowing all things, knows this simple yearning of ours, and from this is born the greatest act of love the world has ever known. For God so loved the world that God gave himself a body that we could see and touch and love in ways familiar to us. The Word was made man, moved among us as a human being, understanding and meeting halfway the limits of how we can love things. The world was in darkness and it saw a great light, a love that rose like the sun above all our sorry shadows of unknowing. The tarot's Sun teaches us about this humbling act of love, the ways in which the Incarnation changed us and changed the world and changes it still.

It would have been very easy, and would have made a certain kind of sense, for God to have appeared to us in great majesty, throwing the weight of his power around like some heavyweight divinity. Christ Incarnate could have been a warrior or a king, a man with the earthly power to match his Godly power. The Incarnation was not an act of power, though. It was an act of love, pure and heartbreakingly simple. God did not come into the world to hold dominion over us. God came into the world as an innocent babe with the purest of intentions. This is what the Sun shows us, God in the form of a child, a boy small and helpless but joyful nevertheless. This is Christ, offering us the naturally reciprocal confidence of a child, the sweetest supposition that he loves us and so we will love him in return.

The love of God broke into the world like the sun at dawn, and darkness prevailed no longer. This love, so pure and innocent, sanctified everything in creation. There is a physicality to tarot's Sun card, an earthiness in its imagery: the sun itself, the flowers, the blood-red banner, the horse, the naked child. God chose to be born straight into all of this, and God could not possibly enter into the world and not make it new in every way. Every tree and rock and flower was touched and redeemed by the love of God flooding over it like the light of the sun at each new day. In the hairsbreadth moment Christ was born, the secular had new potential to be made sacred. Divinity came into the world.

Divinity still lives here now. Christ's physical presence on earth changed the world, but it was not a singular act. The miracle of the Incarnation is that it continues to change the world, day after day. Every square inch of the world is touched by God, and we cannot escape this grace any more than we escape the rising of the sun each day. All things have been filled with the love of God, and we cannot run from it. The presence of God in the world changes us whether we want it to or not. God begets his Son to us whether we like it or not. We may not have asked for this grace, but we got it. Intolerable though it may feel sometimes, God is in this whole sorry and complicated mess of life right here with us. We can come to know God through this life, because the world in which we live is so touched by him. He lets us love him in this way; we get to love him right here where we are. We get to see these ordinary and simple things in the light of the love that changes all things.

REFLECTIONS

- Do you feel as if God is as present in your life as the rising and the setting of the sun each day? Why or why not?
- Reflect on the idea that God could have been born in majesty and chose instead to be born into humility. What does that teach us about the importance of humility?
- Jesus Christ no longer walks the earth, but the presence of the Incarnation remains in our world. Where in your life do you feel the divine intimacy of the Incarnation? Where in your life do you feel like you can touch God?
- Do you feel as if the world is a sacred place, permeated by God's love? Why or why not?

- Spend some time with the idea that God gave his Son to the world out of love for you. If you truly lived each day with the knowledge of that love, how might it change your life?
- Do you feel as if you love God with the same simplicity with which God loves you? If not, how can you lean into the simplicity of love?

JUDGEMENT

Listen, I will tell you a mystery! We will not all die, but we will all be changed, in a moment, in the twinkling of an eye, at the last trumpet. For the trumpet will sound, and the dead will be raised imperishable, and we will be changed. (1 Corinthians 15:51–52)

The final line of the Nicene Creed instructs us to "look forward to the resurrection of the dead." As Christians, we believe that there will be a Last Judgment for which we will all be resurrected. The trumpets' blasts will wake us up, and we will be alive in a way we have never been before. The tarot's Judgement depicts this apocalyptic moment, the eye-opening, veil-rending earthquake of being truly awake for the first time. It is awful, in both senses of the word. We will stand naked before God, we will answer to God alone, and we will go to heaven or we will go to hell. This being the end of the line, there will be no room for maneuvering, no hedging of bets, no way of disguising ourselves from what we have done. Our eyes will be opened to who we are in truth, and God, ever merciful, will forgive every fault if we choose to let him. This is the final destiny of the soul, to be reckoned with God once and for all.

The Last Judgment is a true apocalypse. It is an ending, but is also an uncovering, and we see this in tarot's Judgement. The people in this image are being awakened from a long and death-like sleep, and they are naked. The moment of the Last Judgment is the moment when we will see ourselves as we truly are, with no pretense to hide behind. We will see ourselves in perfectly naked truth. And in that perfectly naked truth, we will find ourselves wanting. Who would not find themselves wanting in the presence of God himself? In this way, tarot's Judgement is a sort of penance on a cosmic scale, less a universal meting out of punishment than a universal confession. We will see ourselves and our faults with bitter clarity, and God will be present to offer absolution.

God will judge us on the Last Day; this thought is terrifying. No one will stand before God and find themselves worthy of God's grace. God will offer it all the same, though, because God's nature always bends toward mercy. Christ on the cross opens his arms to embrace the whole world, and the book of Ephesians tells us that Christ's "plan for the fullness of time" is "to gather up all things in him" (Ephesians 1:10). God wants us all to be as close to God as we can bear to be. On the Last Day, we will see all our faults in the light of scandalous truth, but forgiveness is always ours to accept. It is freely offered to every single one of us by a God who is infinitely irresistible but also a God who will not overpower our freedom to resist. We are gifted with that monstrous gift of free will, and we can use it to the last moments of time eternal. We will open our arms to heaven or we will slam the doors of hell in God's face, but we ourselves will choose.

Who would say no to that kind of mercy? In truth, we do not know, but tarot asks how anyone could. Waite-Smith's exquisite and heart-rending depiction of the Last Judgment shows every single person wide awake and naked and stretching their arms to heaven, begging for the mercy of God. Hell must exist if we are to have the option to refuse God, but tarot's Judgement suggests that hell may well be empty. No one is excluded from accepting salvation; God does not want anyone to be in hell. Maybe no one is, and what a scandalous thought. If we can see judgment in this way—not as condemnation but as eternity's great moment of forgiveness—it becomes not the stuff of nightmares but an eye-opening invitation to closeness. Judgment can be an occasion for joy if we let it. We can be changed, too. All we have to do is throw open our arms and accept the terrible and undeserved mercy of God.

REFLECTIONS

- Reflect on your associations with the Last Judgment. Does it make you feel fearful or hopeful? Do you look forward to the "resurrection of the dead"? Why or why not?

- How might it change your life to spend more time meditating on the Last Judgment, to view your own life in the light of this cosmic, apocalyptic event? Would it change the way you live?

- Reflect on the idea that God is eager to forgive all of your sins. How does it feel?

- Reflect on the idea that God is eager to forgive everyone's sins, even the worst of them. How does *that* feel?
- Do you feel as if the Last Judgment can be seen as an occasion of joy, waking from a dream into a reality that is merciful rather than terrifying? Why or why not?
- In tarot's Judgement, the people are woken up by the trumpet's blast. What in your life has been a trumpet blast for you, a wake-up call to a new and better and more sanctified way of life? How did it change you?

THE WORLD

He has made known to us the mystery of his will, according to his good pleasure that he set forth in Christ, as a plan for the fullness of time, to gather up all things in him, things in heaven and things on earth. (Ephesians 1:9–10)

There is a theory that the word "religion" comes from the Latin *religare,* meaning "to tie or bind." This etymology implies some acknowledgment of dependency on God. It speaks to this inescapable longing for our lives to mean something more than what we see here, to be bound to something beyond just us. We want, sometimes desperately, to be connected to something larger than ourselves. As Christians, we believe that this longing is fulfilled in God alone, that our nature is complete in God alone, that this longing is a longing for unity with God. We also believe that this fulfillment is within our grasp, that when we die, God will dwell in our souls and we will dwell in God. The tarot's World card speaks to this oneness for which we long, this binding of ourselves to God. The World is the fulfillment of our single, indestructible ardor for God. It is eternal bliss, "a new heaven and a new earth" (Revelation 21:1). In the infinite moment of heaven, God will permeate us with his utter openness, and we will feel, for the first time, true peace and joy. This is the new World for which we are made, and so of course this is the end goal of the Fool's journey. Of course the culmination of a contemplative walk through the tarot would be a point where the unity of Creator and creation is finally clear. Of course the finish line is nothing less than the sweet wholeness of heaven itself.

It is often embarrassing to talk about heaven. The idea of heaven speaks to our deepest, most naked longing; there's no irony to hide behind here. We can only speak about heaven from a place of bald-faced earnestness. To speak about heaven is to bow to the vulnerability of a desire that defines us, yet is wholly mysterious to us as well. Here, in this life, we don't know what heaven will be like. We know that we will be with God, but what does that even mean? What is union with God? What does perfect happiness even look like? The Bible uses many images to describe this: light, peace, a wedding feast, the Father's house, the heavenly Jerusalem. Tarot gives us yet another: a figure dancing in eternal rhythm with God, framed by the symbols of the Four Evangelists, who remind us that blissful eternity is the gift of Christ's redemption. As poetic as these images are, they all fall short, because we don't know what heaven will be like. They are still useful, though, inasmuch as they make our longing known, give it a shape with which we can interact. We do not know how heaven will be, but we know we want to be in heaven. We do not know what eternity looks like; we only know that we hope for it beyond all else.

We long for the blissful unity of heaven, but the truth is, heaven often feels a long way off. The perfect promise of tarot's World card can sometimes feel mercilessly unattainable because we do not live in this world, not yet. We do have hope for it, though, and we can let that hope for heaven sustain us. The perfect joy of heaven will be ours, whatever perfect joy may feel like, but in the meantime, we can look for joy here, too. The world we live in here and now is no heaven, but it is a kingdom of joy. Make no mistake, it is also a kingdom of suffering, but the sources of joy are older and deeper and stronger than the sources of suffering. God made the world with joy before suffering was ever introduced. Life is hard, but it is not meaningless, and there are times and places here on earth where heaven can be briefly glimpsed. We can rest in these moments like so many little inns along the road as we journey to our final home. We will find true joy in heaven, but we can seek joy here, too. We will find true unity in heaven, but we can look for unity here on earth, too. We can keep a finger on the pulse of joy, hold fast to the hope of being bound to God, and it will, someday, lead us to that blissful unity of the World.

REFLECTIONS

- Reflect on the ideas about heaven that you see most often. Do they resonate with you? Why or why not?
- Do you feel bound to God? If so, do you feel as if God sometimes tugs at that binding, wanting you to follow him to union? What does that feel like for you?

- The final phrase of the Nicene Creed instructs us to believe "in the life of the world to come." Do you feel like that belief is a central part of your faith? Why or why not?
- Tarot's World card gives us a key to understanding heaven in the symbols of the Four Evangelists. Do you see a glimpse of heaven in the life of Christ? If so, what does that glimpse of heaven look like?
- We are not yet part of the new World of which the tarot speaks, but we can see flashes of it here in this world. Where do you find small glimpses of the joy of heaven here on earth?
- When do you feel closest or most united to God? How does it feel?

5

THE MINOR ARCANA

The minor arcana of the tarot consists of fifty-six cards divided into four suits: Pentacles, Swords, Cups, and Wands. Each suit corresponds to a certain theme. With each of the four suits, I have tried not to stray too far from the original card meanings, instead taking the traditional themes of the suits and looking at them through the lens of Christian theology. The suit of Pentacles, sometimes called the suit of Coins, traditionally speaks to embodiment and what it means to live as a physical being in a physical world; in this book, too, the Pentacles teach us about everyday embodiment and what it means to live as a child in the Father's creation. The suit of Swords, usually concerned with themes of sorrow and misfortune, has things to say about suffering and its place in Christian life. The suit of Cups, conventionally associated with intuition and the unconscious, here is connected to themes of divine love and mercy. The suit of Wands, traditionally linked to themes of fire and passion, teaches us about the Holy Spirit and what it means to be a cocreator with God. The ten cards of each suit carry us through the theme: its frustrations, its beauties, its difficulties, its limitations, its graces. The minor arcana cards are more likely to concern situations we encounter in our daily lives and the choices we have to make. These cards go into finer detail and give us a chance to reflect on the little moments of our lives. Christianity is a big-picture thing, but it is lived out in the small decisions we make each day.

ACE OF PENTACLES

The spirit of God has made me, and the breath of the Almighty gives me life. (Job 33:4)

The story of Christianity begins with the story of Creation. God was and God made. God made the night and the day, the sky and the waters. God made the animals of the air and sea and land. God made the garden of Eden and Adam and Eve. And God rested and declared good all that he had made. We are all intimately familiar with this story, but it is easy to think of it as something removed from us—a poetic story we can tell our children, but hardly something that touches our daily lives. God is still the Creator, though. God created at the beginning of all things, and God creates now. Our lives are no accident, no quirk of fate. With the same infinite power and tender care with which

God made the stars in the sky and the lilies of the valley and the sun that rises on each new day, God has made each one of us. Life itself is a gift, and the Ace of Pentacles is tarot's representation of this gift. It is a reminder that our flesh, our bones, the beat of our hearts and the breath of our lungs and the world in which we live each ordinary moment—they are all gifts from a God who declares us good. This is the original grace, an unfathomable generosity.

To see life in this way, as a specific gift, is a beautiful thought, but in reality, most of life does not feel like an extraordinary miracle. We work, we eat, we sleep, we do the dishes and sweep the floors, walk the dog and water the plants. Much of life is boring. Much of life is drudgery. Much of life feels too ordinary to be a gift. The daily bread is also a gift, though, and the Ace of Pentacles is an exercise in remembering the gift of the ordinary. A pentacle is a humble thing, a talisman or a simple coin. Coins are small and numerous, so mundane as to be almost invisible. They jangle in our pockets. We find them in couch cushions and on sidewalks. This is no fiery wand or victorious sword or overflowing cup. It is a small thing, but God gives us the small things, too, and that's a humbling thought. We can find God in fantastic miracles, but we can also find God in our creatureliness, in the ordinariness of normal life. Holiness dwells in the mundane, too.

The Bible tells us that "even the hairs of your head are all counted" (Luke 12:7). Life may feel ordinary to us, but it is not ordinary to God. This gift of life is a gift of extraordinary care. It is not a gift we can repay; we are creatures to the Creator, and how can a creature repay the gift of its very being? It is, however, a gift for which we can show gratitude, and we do this by taking care with how we order our lives. Nothing in our lives should be an afterthought, even the most ordinary of things. Below the single pentacle, held aloft like a small sun, is a path through a garden, beckoning us to walk through the archway to the mountains beyond. This image encourages us to move fully into the world, the beautiful simplicity of it. The way we walk through this life matters, because this is where we meet God. Our salvation happens in this life, not in some other. It happens in this day, not in some other. It happens in this God-given body, in this God-given world. It matters to God how we use this gift of life. We are pilgrims in this world, and we can walk this way with intention. We can take care with this gift, no matter how small it feels, remembering that it is not mundane to the Creator.

REFLECTIONS

- Reflect on the biblical story of creation. Do you see yourself as a continuation of that story, lovingly made by God? Why or why not?
- Our lives can feel ordinary to us, but they are anything but ordinary to God. How can you accept the gift of life with the same care with which God gives it?
- If you were somehow able to tap into the idea that every single breath you take is a miraculous gift, how might that change your life? Would your days look different? If so, how?
- To acknowledge that life is a gift is to acknowledge that God loves us enough to give us life. How does that feel for you? Is it easy for you to accept that kind of unconditional, unrepayable love? Why or why not?
- We cannot repay God for the gift of life, but we can show gratitude. What are some ways in which you can

show gratitude for the gift of life? How can you use this gift well?

- As a Christian, do you think of the material world as something to be resisted or something to be embraced? Why?

TWO OF PENTACLES

For everything there is a season, and a time for every matter under heaven. (Ecclesiastes 3:1)

Our earthly lives are marked by nothing so much as constant shifting movement. We know joy and we know sorrow. We know work and we know rest. We know clamor and we know silence, each in its turn. Up and down, tension and release. In this way, our lives are like so many little ships riding the mighty waves of life. We cannot attempt to control these rhythms of life without consequence. Though we may try, we cannot stay forever on the crests and we cannot skirt around the troughs. Dancing and mourning, wounding and healing, company and solitude—we cannot escape these things. Though we live in a world in which we are tied to God by our very nature, we are still enmeshed in the vulnerabilities and constraints of creaturely life. How do we live in this world that feels so provisional and improvisatory? What do we do when we just want stability but things are always in flux? How do we seek and determine and follow God's purposes in the midst of the ambiguity of earthly life? The changes and chances of this life happen to us whether we would like them to or not. We cannot control the waves, but we can choose how we ride them, and the Two of Pentacles shows us the most faithful way.

The book of Ecclesiastes reminds us that there is a season for everything. There is a time to work and a time to rest, a time to plant and a time to uproot, a time to tear down and a time to build up. We are stubborn creatures, and we sometimes resist these natural cycles, wanting to cling to the easy seasons and toss out the difficult ones. Our figure in the Two of Pentacles shows us what it looks like to honor this rhythm of life instead of struggle against it. He holds two coins, but he grasps them both lightly, and it almost looks as if he is juggling them. He moves with such ease that he seems to be dancing. There is no fight here. There is no anxiety. There is no struggle to hold on to the season of work or the season of joy. There is no frantic digging in of heels at the prospect of sorrow or fallowness. When it is time to work, he moves into the work. When it is time to rest, he moves into the rest. He dances gracefully in the instability rather than resists it at every turn. We can do this, too. We can take each day as it comes, with its joys and sorrows, its ups and downs. We do not have to fight.

Between the two coins in this image winds a lemniscate, a symbol of eternity. This is the secret of the simple ease we see in the Two of Pentacles. These rhythms of life—rest and work, joy and sorrow, planting and uprooting—they do not stand alone. Every twist and turn is contained within the eternal changelessness of God. All things change, but God never changes, and we are held in this sure knowledge. Our figure in the Two of Pentacles knows this, and this is why he moves with such grace. He recognizes that every movement of his life is held by his Creator, and this is why he dances. He is not weighed down by worldly cares, because all things are held lightly in God's love. Recognizing his creatureliness, he can move lightly here. Trusting in God's care, he can weave in and out of life's rhythms with ease. This is the lesson of the Two of Pentacles: it is only when we are humble enough to recognize our own creatureliness—our own lack of control—that we are able to move freely. When we can trust that we are held by God in each moment, each moment can be held lightly.

REFLECTIONS

- Do you feel as if you move comfortably in the changes of life? Or do you prefer stability, resisting difficult moments and grasping the good moments too tightly? Why?
- What season of life are you in right now? How can you find God there?
- Reflect on the idea that each moment of our lives is held within the eternal changelessness of God. Do you think that idea might make it easier to gain perspective on your life? If so, how? If not, why?
- Are you a person who needs to feel always in control? If so, what are some small things you can do to let go of a little bit of control and instead trust that God holds you like a ship on the sea of life?
- The figure in the Two of Pentacles not only moves in life's changes with ease. He dances. Do you feel like it's

possible for you to move so joyfully in and among the changes of life? Why or why not?

- Is it easier for you to feel God's presence in the easy moments of life or the difficult ones? Why?

THREE OF PENTACLES

For as in one body we have many members, and not all the members have the same function, so we, who are many, are one body in Christ, and individually we are members one of another. (Romans 12:4–5)

In the Bible, the book of Acts tells us about the early church. These new Christians "devoted themselves to the apostles' teaching and to fellowship, to the breaking of bread and the prayers" (Acts 2:42) and were "of one heart and soul" (Acts 4:32). The early church was marked by its sense of community, and this living and working together has been a foundational aspect of Christianity ever since. It is a particularly striking aspect in today's day and age. In the modern world, we are often taught to work hard for our own advancement, to stand out as individuals, to be always concerned about getting our own fair share whether it harms others or not. Christianity preaches something altogether different. We are not meant to find salvation alone. The gospel of rugged individualism holds no sway here. We find holiness in being with others, in learning to work with and for and around other people. The Three of Pentacles shows us the importance of this sense of community in our common life. It is a sacred thing to invest in others and to allow others to invest in us, to learn to be one in heart and soul. When we bear each other up in this life, we can build something greater than the sum of its parts.

In the Three of Pentacles, we see an image of three people working together for a common goal. The artist holds the blueprints, the stonemason carves the stone, the friar prays. Christianity needs visionaries. It needs workers. It needs contemplatives. As Paul tells us, "There are varieties of gifts, but the same Spirit; and there are varieties of services, but the same Lord; and there are varieties of activities, but it is the same God who activates all of them in everyone" (1 Corinthians 12:4–6). We have gifts to give, and we have gifts to receive, and it is in community that we learn how to use those gifts in a way that benefits the whole. It is also in community that we learn our own vulnerability as individuals. None of these three figures could complete this project on their own. They are utterly dependent on each other. In our age of disconnect and individualism, this dependency does not always feel comfortable for us, but it is necessary. It is in this vulnerability—it is in this true community—that we find God. When we are open about our own weaknesses and our own strengths, we learn to honestly depend on others for generosity just as we depend on God for generosity. Here is where we learn just how much we are bound together.

The people in the Three of Pentacles are working together to build a cathedral. The Gothic-style cathedrals of the Middle Ages took at least fifty years to build, and many took much longer than that. It was not uncommon for cathedrals to be built over several hundred years, a process that involved generations of architects and workers. These buildings lasted, though, and they last still. These figures in the Three of Pentacles have committed to a life-time of work that will stand the test of time. There is a deep and reliable stability here, and it is a reminder that we cannot enjoy the sense of unity that the Three of Pentacles promises unless we are committed to the long view of the work. This card teaches us a lesson about finding a place and staying there, working and grow-ing with a community of people—specifically, the same people. What would it look like for us to do this? What would it look like for us to commit to a lifetime of growth in holiness that is bound up in one community? What would it look like to share our gifts with the same people, day in and day out, and to let them share their gifts with us? It is not an instant gratification, and it is not easy work, but it is worth it.

REFLECTIONS

- Do you see the spiritual life as something that is primarily private or communal? Why?
- Are you an active part of a Christian community? If not, why? If so, in what ways do you feel that your community helps you grow in faith?
- Do you feel more comfortable helping others or being helped by others, lifting others up or being lifted up? Why?
- Reflect on the idea that our salvation is meant to be worked out in community with other people, that we

are meant to find holiness together. How does that make you feel?

- What specific gifts do you feel that you have to offer Christianity? (Don't be too modest here! Everyone has a gift worthy of sharing.)
- Many of us have cultivated community in online spaces. Do you feel like virtual community can build the sort of long-term stability seen in the Three of Pentacles? If not, why? If so, what might that look like?

FOUR OF PENTACLES

And he said to them, "Take care! Be on your guard against all kinds of greed; for one's life does not consist in the abundance of possessions." (Luke 12:15)

We are material beings in a material world; it makes sense for us to crave material stability. The instinct for comfort and security is an understandable one, but we so easily take things too far; there is a reason the Bible has so much to say about greed. The Four of Pentacles shows us this instinct for material comfort, and it shows us what happens when it runs unchecked, bearing down on every aspect of one's life. The man in the Four of Pentacles has great material wealth. He wears sumptuous robes and a golden crown; this is the pleasure of *stuff*. And yet, in the same image, we see the shadowy anxiety of avarice. This man has so much, and yet he clings to the coin at his chest, almost curling himself around it. His feet rest on two more, as if to keep them from sliding away. Another is absurdly balanced on his head. There is great wealth here, but there is also a deep uneasiness. The Four of Pentacles asks us to consider what it does to us to spend our lives placing our faith and effort in earthly treasures. This man has dedicated his life to building up material security, but at what cost? And is it worth it?

In the Gospel of Luke, Jesus tells a parable about a rich fool. One year, a wealthy man brings forth a particularly abundant harvest. The man responds to this abundance with grasping greed. He immediately decides that the only course of action is to tear down his existing barns and build bigger ones to hold all his riches, dreaming all the while about the fun he will have with his new and greater wealth. This parable is startling in its sense of isolating self-centeredness. The rich fool spends the entire parable talking to himself and thinking of himself and planning for himself. There are no other characters in the story, until God speaks to the man directly, condemning his greed. We see this same warped, grasping self-focus in the Four of Pentacles. In centering his own desire for material security, the man in this image has completely isolated himself from his community. There is a city behind him, but he sits outside the walls. Tied up in safeguarding his own possessions above all else, he has literally turned his back on his neighbor. There is no communion here, only self-enhancement and the stifling loneliness of greed.

In the Four of Pentacles, we see wealth, but we see no joy. This can be surprising for us, who live in a culture of constant and overwhelming advertisement. Over and over again, we are told in a million different ways that if we just buy the right thing, we will be happy and we will be loved and we will be at peace. The man in the Four of Pentacles has bought everything, but there is no happiness or love or peace to be found here. What we see instead is plenty of fear: fear that his wealth will be taken away, fear that he does not have enough, fear that what he does have will surely be lost. Here is a man who is so very rich in material wealth but so very poor in spiritual goodness. He has not yet internalized that most paradoxical of Christian teachings, that it is in giving that we receive. It is in letting go of our grasping need for security that we find joy. It is in sharing all we have that we store up treasures in heaven and "take hold of the life that really is life" (1 Timothy 6:19), as Paul tells us. Everything we gain in this life is a gift from God, meant to be held lightly and shared with all, lest we be left with a lonely, fallow life.

REFLECTIONS

- Do you relate to the man in this image? Have you ever felt a sense of possessiveness around material things, either out of greed or fear or a sense of scarcity? If so, what did that feel like?

- Think about the times in your life when you felt true joy. Are those moments centered around materiality or community? Why?

- When we think of greed, we usually think of material wealth, but greed can show up in other places in our lives as well. Are there any aspects of your life that you feel immoderately attached to? If so, what would it feel like for you to let go?

- How can you cultivate more courageous generosity in your life? How can you create a sense of selflessness?

- Reflect on the idea that greed separates us from our communities. In what ways can you intentionally care for your community as a way to safeguard against greed and create a spirit of giving in your life?
- We live in a world that constantly tells us that we need more. What are some small ways in which you can push back against our modern culture of materialism?

FIVE OF PENTACLES

When you pass through the waters, I will be with you;
and through the rivers, they shall not overwhelm you;
when you walk through fire you shall not be burned,
and the flame shall not consume you. (Isaiah 43:2)

We can turn to nearly any page in the Bible and find the most faithful people encountering immense struggles: Joseph being sold into slavery by his brothers, the Israelites wandering in the desert for forty years before finding the promised land, Peter weeping after denying Jesus. Job, known for both his great faith and his terrible suffering, has an entire book of the Bible dedicated to his particular troubles. We know that we can turn to God during moments of intense pain and dramatic suffering, but what about the small moments of struggle? What about the little annoyances?

What about the flat tires and the kids with colds and the guy who cut you off in traffic on your way to work this morning? To be a human is to have a hard time. It is to live a life filled with many small joys and an equal number of small crises. Our creaturely selves are lovingly brought into this world, but it is a material world limited by so many little slings and arrows of misfortune. The Five of Pentacles offers us an honest image of all the sorry sufferings we bear in this life, the suffering we cannot escape. It also offers us, though, a lesson in how to live faithfully in the midst of it.

While we instinctively turn to God in moments of great sorrow, we don't always do so in the smaller, more daily moments of frustration. When our struggles are small, it is easy to convince ourselves that we shouldn't bother God about them, that God somehow has more important things to do than listen to our petty problems. We think that we can handle the little difficulties on our own, and perhaps we can, but we do not have to. It is a prideful thing to push away the love of God, to prefer the illusion of independence and self-sufficiency to the terrifying ordeal of accepting help. The Five of Pentacles asks us if it might be easier to live into our weakness rather than try to hold it all together. The two people in this image are beggars. They are, by definition, dependent on the mercy of others for their own well-being, not just sometimes but all the time. We are used to leaning on God when we walk through the valley of the shadow of death, but we can lean on God in the small moments of suffering as well. We can lean on God in every moment. We can live in a posture of ceaseless humility. We can live as beggars before God, always needing mercy and always receiving it.

The beggars of the Five of Pentacles are walking in the snow, and above them is a stained-glass window. An image of pure abundance, five coins form the shape of a tree around which wind fertile grapevines. It is a golden light standing out in the darkness, inviting the beggars into the warmth of sanctuary. The Five of Pentacles is an image of suffering, but it is also an image of safety. One of the great comforts of the Christian faith is that our God is present with us in the moments of deep suffering, to be sure, but also in the million little things that can go wrong every day; his sacred proximity is always available to us. The promise of God is not that we will never suffer, but that no injury or illness or distress will have complete power over us. The holy anoints all the poor, sorry moments of our lives. This is the secret of the Five of Pentacles, that God keeps us equally safe in sorrow and in joy if we are humble enough to bring our troubles to him. We may despair many things, but never need we despair of the mercy of God.

REFLECTIONS

- Do you feel as if you are in a period of sustained suffering in your life right now? Do you relate to this image? In what ways does it draw you in?
- Do you feel comfortable accepting help from people when you're struggling? Or do you prefer to handle things on your own, especially when your struggles feel small in comparison with others? Why or why not?
- Reflect on the humility that the Five of Pentacles asks of us. What emotional reaction do you have to being seen as a beggar in the eyes of God?
- Do you believe that God wants to help us in our suffering, even with the small, daily struggles? Why or why not?
- Put yourself in this image of the Five of Pentacles. Would you enter the church? If so, what might that

feel like for you? If not, what would it feel like to stay outside?

- The Five of Pentacles shows us an image of God's presence as warmth and light and safety. Do you relate to that sense of divine presence? What does the presence of God feel like for you?

SIX OF PENTACLES

... for I was hungry and you gave me food, I was thirsty and you gave me something to drink, I was a stranger and you welcomed me. (Matthew 25:35)

Jesus spent his time on earth healing suffering in deeply physical ways. He used touch, spit, wine, and bread to heal the sick, feed multitudes, and express his love for us. These were acts of spiritual healing, but they were also more than that. Jesus was divine, but Jesus was also human, and he spent his earthly life giving human comfort to human people. In following Jesus's example, we are commanded to do the same. It is the heart of Christianity to love one's neighbor as oneself. We are made to care for one another, and we are creatures in need of creaturely comfort, so our care must be more than prayer. It must be care that can be seen and touched, heard and tasted. We are called to wash, feed, clothe, heal as often as we can, with every person we meet. We see this giving, simultaneously physical and sacred, in the Six of Pentacles. In a tender image of charity, a merchant gives to two beggars. He does not pass by. He does not abdicate his responsibility to his neighbor by flippantly offering thoughts and prayers. He does not stop to consider whether or not they deserve his charity. He has much to offer, and he gives it freely. Jesus made it quite clear that this is how we are to love each other. It is uncomplicated, and it is holy.

Love is a reciprocal action. We are called to give love, but we are also called to receive it, and so while it is perhaps most comfortable to see ourselves in the position of the generous merchant, we must also see ourselves in the dependency of the beggars. Jesus understood this need well; he taught us how to offer care, but he also taught us how to receive it. He spent his life caring for others, but he was also dependent on others for generosity. Jesus did not hold people at arms' length but gratefully accepted gifts, friendship, hospitality. He took care of people, but he also allowed himself to be taken care of. In this way, he showed us what love looks like. It is a sharing of God's gifts with others, but it is also living in grateful dependence on God's gifts given by other people. Like Jesus, we are meant to live in vulnerable assumption of mutual need and generosity. We cannot always be the person who gives, and while we do not always like to see ourselves in the person who needs, this is who we are. The Creator gives and the created receive, and so to be a Christian is to give with grace, but it is also to receive with grace.

With one hand extended in a traditional gesture of divine blessing, the merchant gives the beggars gold. With his other hand, he holds a scale, connecting his giving to the virtue of justice. The Six of Pentacles teaches us that charity and justice are intimately connected. It is common to think of charity as a private act, something in which we can choose to indulge when we feel so moved, but Christianity tells us that this mutual giving and receiving is actually the only just way to live. When Jesus walked through the world offering and receiving physical comfort, he was practicing justice. It was a justice rooted not in retribution but in love and relationship. Jesus taught us that true justice lies in the recognition that God the Creator has provided ample gifts for all creatures, and so true justice is being willing to share one's gifts with the knowledge that God will provide. If we truly believe this, then we must also believe that communal sharing is not to be done only when we feel inspired to do so, but freely and generously and constantly. We are called to participate in dependence and receptivity in physical, material ways. This is the loving mutuality at the heart of creaturely existence.

REFLECTIONS

- In this image, do you see yourself more in the merchant or the beggars? Why?
- Reflect on the idea that Jesus spent his earthly life not just performing miracles but also offering earthly comfort. Does it change how you see Jesus to reflect on his humanity in that way? If so, in what ways?
- When you offer care to people, do you first stop to consider whether or not they deserve it? Or do you give freely and without judgment as the merchant in the Six of Pentacles? Why?
- Reflect on the idea that Jesus taught us how to give care, but also how to receive it. Which do you feel more comfortable with, personally? Why?

- What are some concrete ways in which you can practice the mutual generosity of justice seen in the Six of Pentacles?
- What tangible, physical caretaking can you give to those you love?
- What tangible, physical caretaking would you like to receive?

SEVEN OF PENTACLES

Remember the sabbath day, and keep it holy.
(Exodus 20:8)

The first six days of the Genesis creation story are nothing but one heart-stopping miracle after another. Night and day, sky and sea, plants and animals, Adam and Eve—they are not there, and then they are. God lovingly fashions an entire universe, utterly poetic, from the microcosmic to the macrocosmic. And then, on the seventh day of creation, God rests. Reality itself is created in a magnificent cascade of power, and then God takes a break. Most of us are so familiar with this story that we only half-hear it, but this day of rest should be a spiritual shock to us. Gods do not rest, but our God does, and he invites us into this rest as well. This is the Sabbath. It is a space of necessary passivity and an essential element of our relationship with the Creator. We are literally commanded to remember the Sabbath and keep it holy. We are called to set aside time to remove ourselves from our day-to-day lives, to deliberately put ourselves into God's time and God's presence. The Seven of Pentacles is tarot's representation of the Sabbath. A gardener has worked, and now he takes a slow and unhurried breath.

Rest does not always come easily for us. We live in an age when time is money and efficiency reigns supreme and productivity is the highest virtue. How much can we get done in the least amount of time? How can we squeeze the most out of every minute of work? How can we make even our leisure *useful* in some way? Our highest goal is doing the very most as often as possible. In the context of this workaholic culture, the slowness of the Sabbath can seem quaintly archaic. Modern eyes look at the gardener in this image and see laziness, a wasting of time. This gardener could be weeding his garden. He could be watering his plants. He could be planning future crops. Instead, he is doing precisely nothing. This is the radical rest of the Sabbath. It is our chance to pull out of our modern ideas of seeing all time in terms of usefulness. It allows us to step outside of the perpetual motion machine of our daily lives and the economic structure that insists we always be working. In commanding the Sabbath, God commands us to set aside our anxious productivity. This is no easy task, but if we can manage to do this, it puts all the little hurried complications of our lives into a larger perspective. We are more than what we can do in each moment, and there is holiness in not-doing. This is sacred rest, and it creates space for worship.

The worship does not always come easily for us, either, though. Worship implies a certain humility, a recognition that God is more powerful than we are. It reminds us that we are not the center of the universe. We see this humbling and destabilizing perspective in the Seven of Pentacles. This gardener seems to be a good gardener. If the healthy growth of his vine is any indication, he spends much time tending his garden. He obviously takes his work seriously. On six days of the week, he extends control over every aspect of his garden, and he is the lord of his plot of land. But on the Sabbath, he does not rule over creation. On the Sabbath, he sees himself as a part of God's creation. This is why, in this image, the gardener and his vine are both in the foreground and take up roughly the same amount of space. This is what the Sabbath does for us. It presses our noses against a different order of the universe, one that does not have us at the center. In our holy pause, we are thrust into the remembrance that we are a part of the world as everything else is. This is where worship happens, at the moment when we remember and acknowledge that we are not the gardeners but the gardened. We can rest in the fact that we are not the makers, but the made.

REFLECTIONS

- Do you observe the Sabbath? If so, how do you make the Sabbath feel different from the other six days of the week?
- Is it easy for you to carve out space for Sabbath rest in your life? Or does the busyness of your life press in? If busyness feels inescapable, why might that be?
- Place yourself in the position of the figure in the Seven of Pentacles. Would you feel as comfortable as he does resting from labor? Or would you feel pressured to do something productive? Why?
- Reflect on the idea that the Sabbath is a reminder that we are not the masters of our own fates, that we are as

much a part of God's creation as anything else. How does that make you feel?

- The Sabbath is a chance to see our lives from God's perspective rather than our own. Do you ever allow yourself to see your life in that way? How do you think it might feel?
- What are some concrete ways in which you can honor the Sabbath each week? How can you pull yourself out of your day-to-day life and into God's time? How can you allow yourself that rest?

EIGHT OF PENTACLES

Therefore, my beloved, be steadfast, immovable, always excelling in the work of the Lord, because you know that in the Lord your labor is not in vain. (1 Corinthians 15:58)

Saint Francis received the stigmata. Teresa of Ávila had a vision of being pierced by a mystical arrow of love. Moses heard God in a burning bush. It is easy to see holiness in the drama of stories like these. Some moments are obviously sacred, suffused with a miraculous sense of God's presence and purpose. Perhaps some of us have had our own mystical experiences of God, moments when we felt pulled out of our ordinary lives and into the extraordinary. These are only moments, though, and no one's life is so dramatic all of the time. Most of our days are, by definition, awfully ordinary.

Boring, even. So what do we do with the boring days? How do we find holiness *here,* amid the sameness of our lives? The Eight of Pentacles tells us that is possible, and even necessary, for our lives of faith. Here is a man going about his daily work. His work is not grand and dramatic. There are no mystical visions or miraculous acts here. This is one simple and ordinary day among many simple and ordinary days, but there is a deep faithfulness here as well. The Eight of Pentacles is a reminder that holiness can be found in the little labors of the everyday. Indeed, that is where it must be found, because a faith built only on mountaintop experiences is no faith at all.

Our man in the Eight of Pentacles is not an artist, but a craftsman. He is surrounded by coins, and each one is exactly the same. The craftsman's job is to show up, day after day, to put in the same kind of work. This is an image of habit, and it is a reminder that the path to holiness is often painfully undramatic. We all love stories of mystical visions and grand acts of saintly heroism, and of course those stories have their places in the history of Christianity. But holiness—a life of faith—is built in habits. So much of being a good person involves simply showing up each day and doing our work with love. We go to church on Sundays, even if we do not feel particularly holy when we do so. We wake up each morning and pray, even when prayer feels dry. We treat our neighbors with gentleness and grace, even if we receive no accolades for it. These are the small coins we fashion, each one a gift. It isn't particularly exciting, but our lives need not be dramatic to be holy. The Bible tells us that God will "bless all your undertakings" (Deuteronomy 28:12), and we must believe that God blesses the small undertakings, too. What the Eight of Pentacles teaches us is that the Christian life is not a series of miraculous encounters with God, but rather a long apprenticeship in holiness.

All that being said, there is a paradoxical lesson hidden in the

Eight of Pentacles. Look at the craftsman. There is such an easy rhythm to his work. His expression is peaceful. He is not frantically hurrying to make more coins. He is not resentfully trudging through the process. He is gratefully, contentedly showing up to each day's labor. In doing so, he is placing himself directly in the present moment, in the silent and relaxed posture of contemplation. This is the craftsman's great secret. At the center of his work—work that seems to us so boring from the outside—is an awareness of eternity. He knows that if he perceives Christianity as an endless search for mystical encounters with God, he will surely be disappointed. He also knows that the only trick to the contemplative life is to make space for it in the first place. If we can do the same—if we can accept and sink into the habits of faithfulness instead of resist them—we are much more likely to encounter God. The Eight of Pentacles, with its quiet craftsman, invites us to see how the heart, buried in the mundane habits of faithfulness, can find the sacred potential.

REFLECTIONS

- Reflect on your perception of Christianity. Do you think of it as a religion of chasing after encounters with God? Or as a life of faithful habits? Why?
- What sustains you in your faith? Is it mountaintop moments? Or is it smaller and more mundane things? Why?
- What are your habits of faithfulness?
- The Eight of Pentacles teaches us about remaining steadfast in our faith even when faith doesn't feel exciting. Do you feel like this is something you're

good at? Or do you struggle with the habits of faith when they feel dry? Why?

- 1 Thessalonians 5:17 encourages us to "pray without ceasing." What does that mean to you? Do you think that the contemplative nature of the Eight of Pentacles could help you learn to pray without ceasing, to remain connected to eternity even in the mundane moments of life?

- Reflect on the idea of Christianity as a lifelong apprenticeship. Does that idea shift your perception of faith? If not, why? If so, in what ways?

NINE OF PENTACLES

O taste and see that the Lord is good. (Psalm 34:8)

God created the world out of sheer inexhaustible love for us; everything we know is a gift from a God who loves us beyond any understanding. If we truly believe this, then it follows that enjoying the gift should be a priority in our lives. Pleasure should be a priority in our lives. It is not always, though. Christianity has a history of keeping pleasure at arm's length as a way to avoid sin and the near occasion of it. After all, one of our religion's most famous stories is about a woman who ate something she was not supposed to eat, took pleasure that was not hers to take. There is a difference, though, between stubborn abstinence and thoughtful moderation. It is the difference between fearfully rejecting a gift and gratefully accepting it with a promise to enjoy it. The Nine of

Pentacles asks us what would happen if we accepted pleasure as our birthright from God, if we truly believed that we could taste and see the goodness of the Lord. What if there is a way to experience pleasure in this life that is not only healthy but virtuous? What if, through this way, we can love God and love ourselves? What if we are made for this, too?

The Nine of Pentacles is an image of radiant abundance. Here is a noblewoman dressed in fine robes, standing among lush grapevines, surrounded by golden coins. This woman is immersed in a scene of overwhelming bounty, and yet the tension of temptation is noticeably absent. Here we see only pleasurable relaxation. This pleasure? It is worship. Worship can be solemn and serious and spiritual, but it can also be light and cheerful and physical. We can worship through confession and petition and repentance, but we can also worship through pleasure. It is worship to savor a good meal. It is worship to dress oneself with care. It is worship to stand in a garden and feel the sun on one's face. It is worship to taste and see that the Lord is good. God is a Mother who has given her children a gift. God wants her creation to be enjoyed, and to do so should not be an afterthought in the Christian life. The Nine of Pentacles suggests that it is not more pious to allow all pleasure to be locked away by scrupulous ideas about what is best for one's soul. Our creaturely existence is a gift, and we can know and love God through the joys our existence brings us.

There is a difference between pleasure for pleasure's sake and pleasure for God's sake. We are not called to the former. The woman in the Nine of Pentacles enjoys the gift of God's creation, but she never slips into hedonism. On her left hand perches a hooded falcon, a symbol of self-control. The Nine of Pentacles is an image of pleasure, but it is a temperate pleasure. For many of us, the word "temperance" calls to mind images of strict sobriety, but that does the virtue a disservice. To be temperate is to moderate one's pleasures so as not to be overcome by them. It is, in a sense, a sort of self-love, inasmuch as it teaches us to treat ourselves and our environments with care, to not abuse either. We see this in the Nine of Pentacles. This woman carries herself with such poise and serenity, and she is able to do this because she understands her own inherent dignity as a child of God. Here is a woman who lives in the world, ignoring neither her body nor her soul. Instead, she lives in a balance, ruled neither by pleasure nor by the fear of pleasure. She enjoys the gift of life, she reflects that enjoyment back to God in gratitude, and she teaches us to do the same.

REFLECTIONS

- Do you see the material world as something that helps you to feel connected to God? Or do you see it as something that keeps you from God? Why?
- Reflect on your relationship with pleasure. Is it easy for you to take pleasure in things? Or does it feel difficult? Why?
- Reflect on the idea that God genuinely wants you to enjoy your life, in the same way a mother wants to see her children live happy lives. Is it easy for you to accept that idea? Or do you see God in a different way? Why?
- How do you experience worship? Have you ever thought about pleasure as worship, as an act of gratitude for the gift of life? If not, how might that change your experience of worship?
- The woman in the Nine of Pentacles is able to truly enjoy her life, and she's able to do this because she

practices the virtue of temperance; she controls her pleasure, not the other way around. Have you ever thought about pleasure in this way, as being more enjoyable when practiced in moderation? If so, how did that change your relationship to pleasure?

- Spend some time thinking about something in your life that brings you pleasure: going on a hike, playing with your dog, eating a really good meal, taking a nap. The next time you do that, try seeing it as an act of worship. How do you think it might feel?

TEN OF PENTACLES

But the steadfast love of the Lord is from everlasting to everlasting on those who fear him, and his righteousness to children's children. (Psalm 103:17)

The Bible is full of genealogies. These long accounts of who begat whom—these seemingly endless lists of ancient names—are easy to skip over in favor of more dramatic biblical tales. After all, what will we learn from slogging through verse upon verse of family trees? What do these old ancestral threads have to teach us? A lot, as it turns out. The Bible contains these genealogies for a reason; there is a sacred lesson in the naming of these names. Each one of us has been made carefully and lovingly by the Creator, and while each one of us is loved by God as an individual, Christianity is not a religion of individualism. It is a religion of family. We, who are so loved by God, are a part of a long legacy of people who are loved by God. We are a part of these genealogies, too. The Ten of Pentacles shows us what it looks like to be a part of the family of faith. This is a crowded image of multiple generations: an old man, his children, his children's children. Every member of this family stands under the same arch, lives in the same home, is connected to and relies on the others in small but holy ways. The Ten of Pentacles is a reminder that the whole point of our creaturely lives is to find ways to belong to each other, and in so doing, to belong to God as well.

It is notable that, in the Ten of Pentacles, our eyes are not drawn to any one person in particular but to the image as a whole. What we see most easily is not the people themselves so much as the connections between them. The old man pets a dog and watches his older children, who are in conversation with each other. A young child clings to his mother while petting the dog. Each person has a place and a part within the family and is deeply connected to the others. These connections between the members of the family offer us a glimpse of a deep dependence. This may be uncomfortable for us, as Western culture idolizes the exact opposite, endlessly praising individualism and independence and freedom of self. There is none of that here, though. There is only a group of people who see mutual care as more important than personal liberty, who see themselves as part of a corporate self. The ten coins in this image are dispersed throughout the scene, because everyone has coins to give and everyone has coins to receive. No one stands outside the family, and each member has something to offer to the others. Within the context of the family of faith, our goal in life is to offer what we can contribute and to receive what we need in turn. In doing so, we sink ever further into receptive dependence within the family of creation.

There is a deep thread of humility in the Ten of Pentacles,

a sense of living into the smallness of one individual life. None of the figures in this image are trying to prove they are special, because their specialness comes precisely from their relatedness to the others. The glory of the Ten of Pentacles is that we get to be a part of a larger whole. Look at the old man in this image. He wears a beautifully woven cloak. No single thread in this cloak looks like much all on its own. But woven together, they make something astonishingly beautiful. The Ten of Pentacles invites us to pull back and see our lives within this larger context, to look at our lives through the eyes of God rather than the eyes of man, to see ourselves as a part of the genealogy of faith. To share in God's blessing is to expand our horizon beyond ourselves and beyond our lives to embrace a bigger cosmic story. Our lives might feel small, but we are a part of a wisdom that stretches back for generations.

REFLECTIONS

- Do you think of Christianity as a religion of family and community? Has that been your experience of Christianity? Why or why not?
- Reflect on the idea that you are, through the love of God, connected to every other person in creation. How does that feel for you, to know that you are a part of the family of things?
- Do you think your family has things to teach you about faith? What do you think your ancestors might have to teach you? What lessons might the children in your family have for you?

- Do you feel like you have a place in the family of God? What might your own thread bring to the tapestry of faith?

- The Ten of Pentacles reminds us that our own small lives are part of a much larger divine story. Does that make your life feel more important to you or less? Why?

- What are some concrete ways in which you can foster a sense of connection with people in your religious community? How can you tap into that sense of the family of faith?

ACE OF SWORDS

Rejoice insofar as you are sharing Christ's sufferings,
so that you may also be glad and shout for joy when
his glory is revealed. (1 Peter 4:13)

Suffering is, in many ways, inseparable from who we are as human
beings. We cannot fully shield ourselves from it, no matter how
hard we try. We cannot run away from it, for it will always make
itself known. Sharp and inescapable, it coexists with us in the
world. The Ace of Swords is tarot's representation of this suffering,
the great inevitable pain. A sword is a weapon. By definition, it is
a thing that wounds. Suffering pierces us, splits us open, strips us
bare. While it hurts, it does have a kind of value, because suffering
gets to the very marrow of who we are. Like nothing else, it pushes
us to the edge of ourselves and begs us to make it mean some-

thing. It demands to be considered. We do not ask deep existential questions about ourselves and our lives when we are happy and content, but when we suffer, we want to know *why*. Christianity's great gift lies not in shielding us from suffering but in answering the question of suffering. If we study the story of God's people, we will find not one who has walked through life untested. The treasure of our faith is not absence of suffering, but in making the suffering mean something more.

As Christians, we find the answer to suffering in the life of Christ. We worship a God who became fully man and experienced life as we ourselves experience it. Jesus, in his earthly life, knew joy and laughter, peace and love and contentment. But a God cannot be fully man without also experiencing suffering, that thing so particularly essential to the nature of humankind. Christ knew this, and so he entered intimately into our suffering as well as our joy. He entered into life even unto death. This is the deep, paradoxical center of our entire faith. Everything hinges on this mysterious sacrifice. Christ manifested his divine power by suffering with us. Christ manifested his divine greatness in human weakness. We have a God who loves us so much as to be willing to feel the sting of death, the sharp edge of the sword, the deepest hurt we can imagine. Christ's Passion is where human suffering reached its culmination, because the Passion is where suffering was linked to the divine love beyond all understanding. In the cross, human suffering itself is redeemed. It is given meaning. The question of it is answered. This is why the Ace of Swords is simultaneously an instrument of great pain and a symbol of peaceful victory, the sword topped with a golden crown and olive and palm branches. There is pain here, but there is also glory.

All of tarot's Aces are gifts. While it does not do well to think of suffering itself as a gift—it is not a thing we should seek out for its own sake—we can embrace the suffering we will inevitably come across in our lives. The gift is not the suffering but the meaning that comes from it. The gift is the way suffering can transform us when we choose to stop resisting it and to instead unite it with the suffering of Christ. This is obviously an easy thing to commit to and an exceedingly difficult thing to actually do. Our natural impulse is to flee from suffering, but if we learn to move through it rather than frantically avoid it at all costs, then we learn to handle it differently. We become willing to let it teach us, to see how God uses suffering to open us and change us and draw us closer to him. This is what the Ace of Swords teaches us, and what we see in the cards that follow it. Christ's suffering—God's suffering—invites us to see grace where there is pain, to see resurrection where there is death, to see victory where there is loss. We suffer, and we cause suffering, but Christ conquered death and gave us a crown of joy, and because of that, every moment of suffering can be claimed as a way that leads to new life.

REFLECTIONS

- All of tarot's Aces are blessings, even the suffering Ace of Swords. Is it possible to see suffering as a sort of blessing? Or does that feel unimaginable? Why?
- How do you cope with periods of suffering in your life? Is your first impulse to take your suffering to God? Or is your first impulse something else? Why?
- Do you feel like your faith is something that is supposed to protect you from experiencing suffering? Why or why not?
- The verse from 1 Peter tells us to rejoice that we are able to share in Christ's sufferings. Do you see your

own suffering as a share in Christ's suffering? Would you be able to rejoice in that connection? If so, what might that feel like?

- Do you view the avoidance of suffering to be a main goal in your life? If so, why?
- Spend some time meditating on Christ's Passion. How might holding on to the deep humanity of Christ's suffering change your feelings on your own suffering in this life? Would it make you feel less alone?

TWO OF SWORDS

For those who want to save their life will lose it, and those who lose their life for my sake will save it. (Luke 9:24)

There is a story in the Gospel of Matthew about the mother of James and John asking a favor of Jesus. She brings her two sons to Jesus, and she asks if they might sit at Jesus's right and left hands in his kingdom. In response, Jesus turns to James and John and asks them, "Are you able to drink the cup that I am about to drink?" (Matthew 20:22). Jesus is referring to his Passion and death, which he foretells several times over the course of the Gospel of Matthew. Jesus made it clear that his way was not a way of ease. In this story, he is asking James and John if they are willing to follow him even when it hurts, if they have the courage to drink from his cup. We have the same choice to make. In our lives, we can choose to make the avoidance of suffering our highest goal. Or we can drink from the cup, entering fully into a life with Christ and all that might come with it. The Two of Swords shows us the brink of this choice. A woman sits at the edge of a river, her white dress calling to mind a novitiate or a candidate for baptism. She can choose to stay in this blind, defensive posture, or she can drop the swords and take off her blindfold and open herself to a new kind of life.

This woman sitting on the riverbank is well protected. Her arms are crossed, and she has two sharp swords with which to defend herself. She is blindfolded so as to avoid even the glimpse of a threat. Wearing white, she is an innocent in the literal sense of the word, untouched and unwounded. We can choose to spend our whole lives like this woman, and, indeed, many of us do. We hold on to our innocence, keep suffering at a comfortable distance, remain untouched by suffering ourselves and unseeing of the suffering of others. What do we lose, though, when we live like this? A lot, as it turns out. The woman in the Two of Swords is well defended, but she is also sterile and cold. There is safety here, but there is also fear. In an attempt to protect herself, this woman is also defending herself from intimacy. When we spend our whole lives trying to keep suffering at a distance, we cannot but keep love at a distance as well. No one can hurt us if we're holding two swords, but we also cannot embrace our friends while holding two swords. We cannot hold our children in our arms while holding two swords. We cannot help someone who is hurting while we are holding two swords. To stay in this state of innocence forever is possible, but only at a terrible cost. It is not life at all, but only avoidance of death.

If we try to save our lives, we will only lose them. There is another way, though. In the story from Matthew, James and John tell Jesus that they are able to drink from the cup, and drink from the cup they do. John stays with Jesus until the bitter end, the only one of the twelve apostles present at the crucifixion. James is eventually martyred in Jerusalem by King Herod. James and John lost their surety for the sake of Christ, and in doing so, they gained so much more. Had they not followed Christ, they likely would have led easier lives. They were brave enough, though, to move out of the defensive stalemate of fear and enter fully and faithfully into an unknowable future. The Two of Swords teaches us that there are more profound things to live for than mere safety. We can spend our lives like this woman, sitting on the shore with our arms crossed, afraid of what might happen if we grasp it fully. We can be innocents forever, trying in vain to experience life without the possibility of being hurt by it. But Christ calls us to something bolder and braver than untouched innocence. He calls us to put down the swords and move into the water of life, to be baptized into something new and unknowable. This is how we save our lives.

REFLECTIONS

- Spend some time with the woman in this image. Do you relate to her? If so, in what ways? If not, why?
- Imagine spending your whole life in this position of the Two of Swords. How does that possibility feel? Protective? Stifling?
- The figure in the Two of Swords wears a blindfold to keep herself from seeing the suffering of others. Take an honest look at yourself. Do you do the same? Do you try to keep others' suffering at a distance? Why or why not?

- When moving through life, do you feel more comfortable in a pose of defensiveness or in opening yourself to other people? Why?
- If Jesus asked you directly if you were willing to drink from his cup, what would you say? How would you feel?
- What would you do with your life if you lived fully in faith, if fear and control were not factors, if you held no sword with which to defend yourself?

THREE OF SWORDS

. . . and live in love, as Christ loved us and gave himself up for us, a fragrant offering and sacrifice to God. (Ephesians 5:2)

Jesus moved through his earthly life with an exquisitely tender heart. He healed the sick and fed the hungry and shared meals with outcasts, noticing the people no one else noticed. He loved deeply, and he called us to do the same. The greatest commandment, according to the Gospels, is to love God with everything we have and to love each person we meet as much as we love ourselves. We sometimes like to make our faith more complicated than it is, but it is not really so complicated. Christianity is about love. That is all. We are called, before anything else, to love. We are called to live with open hearts, to love without exception, to care for sinners and saints in equal measure, to turn the other cheek, to bare ourselves over and over again. The Three of Swords is tarot's representation of this vulnerable approach to life. There is no protection for this heart: no walls, no armor, not even a rib cage. There is only an arresting openness, a willingness to move and to be moved. As Christians, we are called to bravely open ourselves to the fullness of life. And brave we must be, because to love in this way is not for the faint of heart.

Make no mistake, this openness will wound us. If we bare ourselves to life, move through our days without a comfortable emotional distance, we will be hurt. There is simply no other way. The hard truth of this vulnerability is embedded in our very language. The word "vulnerable" comes from the Latin *vulnus,* which means "wound." Vulnerability is the capacity to be wounded. To truly love requires exposing oneself to the possibility of being hurt. The Three of Swords does not shy away from letting us know exactly what we are getting ourselves into with this vulnerable approach to life, this love to which we are commanded. The bright red of the heart and the cold gray of the swords do not let us look away from the knowledge that love and suffering are two sides of the same sharp sword, that we cannot have one without the possibility of the other, that there is an intimate connection between the two. This is a stark and almost shocking image, but it is a stark and shocking lesson that this card teaches us. Love hurts. Love hurts, and we have to love anyway.

Our animal instinct tells us to recoil from open wounds. We want to hide them, bandage them, protect them, keep them from happening at all. In the Three of Swords, though, the wounds are proudly displayed, shockingly bared for all to see. In this open woundedness, the image of the Three of Swords bears a striking resemblance to the Sacred Heart, one of the most recognizable symbols of the Christian faith. The Sacred Heart, an image of

Christ's heart aflame with love and pierced with a lance and bound by a crown of thorns, is a visceral expression of Christ's willingness to love at any cost. A symbol of divine love and suffering, the Sacred Heart reminds us that we worship a God of divine woundedness. While the wounds of the Three of Swords are difficult to look at, we should look all the same, because these wounds are sacred proof that we have loved the way Christ instructed us to love. Christ does not call us to innocent hearts. He calls us to wounded hearts. The brokenness of the Three of Swords is nothing less than the unbearable courage of love, and the brokenness itself is what makes us most like the Christ we worship.

REFLECTIONS

- The Three of Swords is one of the most visceral and recognizable cards in the tarot. Spend some time reflecting on your gut reaction to this image. What are the first feelings that come up when you see this card?
- Who in your life do you feel immediately willing to love in the vulnerable way of the Three of Swords? Do you think it's possible to love everyone in this way, as we are called to do? Why or why not?
- Are you familiar with the image of the Sacred Heart? Does that image of divine woundedness speak to you? Why or why not?
- What are some ways in which you can bring this kind of openheartedness into your everyday life? How can you better love people in this way?
- When you love deeply and it leads to suffering, that suffering love is united to Christ's suffering love.

Do you think that idea might help you to love more bravely? If so, how?

- The Three of Swords teaches us that there is strength in vulnerability. When have you embodied this vulnerable strength in your own life?

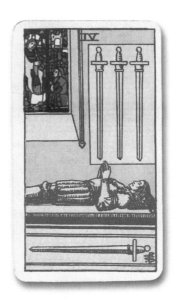

FOUR OF SWORDS

I will both lie down and sleep in peace; for you alone,
O Lord, make me lie down in safety. (Psalm 4:8)

If we love the way Christ tells us to love, we will feel more deeply
than we knew it was possible for a human heart to feel. If we live
the way Christ instructs us to live, we will know great peaks of
love, we will know valleys of the shadow of death, and we will
know every emotional landscape in between. This seems like more
than one heart can bear. How can Christ ask this of us? How
can we possibly live this way and know any sort of peace? If we
try to handle this kind of life on our own, we can't. If we insist
on maintaining an illusion of independence and competency, it
will wear us down to the very edge of our human limitations. In
truth, we cannot live the Christian way without the help of Christ,

and Christ knows this. In the Gospel of Matthew, Jesus tells his followers, "Come to me, all you that are weary and are carrying heavy burdens, and I will give you rest" (Matthew 11:28). The Four of Swords shows us this rest with an image of a quiet and serene chapel. There is a way for us to know this peace. This rest is ours for the taking, but it does require something of us. The Four of Swords shows us the laying down of heavy burdens, but it also shows us the cost.

The Four of Swords shows us a peaceful chapel, and in the chapel is a tomb. The peace of the Four of Swords—the rest that Jesus promises us—is not a surface-level sort of relaxation. This is not taking a break with a bubble bath and a scented candle. This is death. It is a brutal transaction of total surrender. It is raw trust born of desperate need. The Four of Swords pushes us to acknowledge that we cannot rest in God and hold on to our illusions of self-sufficiency at the same time. To place our burdens at the feet of Christ is to kill the false self that we so desperately cling to, the self that believes it can handle life's burdens on its own. In order to give our suffering to Christ, we have to admit that we are suffering. In order for Christ to carry our burdens, we have to hand them over in their entirety. It requires admission of weakness and ceding of control, and that rarely feels good. We can rest in God alone, we can quiet our hearts, and we can know peace, but in order to do this, we must entrust our very lives into the hands of God. Christ will carry our hurts, but we have to let him.

Above the tomb in the Four of Swords is a stained glass window, depicting Christ blessing a person kneeling at his feet. The surrender of self that the Four of Swords insists on can feel like a sort of death, but it can be a blessing, too. The tomb is severe, but the setting is peaceful. Surrender is an act of prayer. It is a sort of devotion. If we can manage it, it will bring us closer to Christ than we ever thought possible. When we are alone with God in the stillness and silence of surrender, we realize that we do not have to handle our lives on our own. In this surrender, we find hope. And in this hope, we find the belief that our suffering in this life will not be the end of us. When we give our burdens to Christ, we find that Christ is indeed able to carry them for us. In this way, surrender is a gift to God, but it is also a gift from God, a gift from the God who knows us better than we know ourselves, who is infinitely more capable of bearing our suffering than we are. When we give God our burdens, we receive love in return. When we surrender into true rest, we find grace.

REFLECTIONS

- Spend some time reflecting on the image of the Four of Swords. What are your initial reactions to it? Does it feel peaceful? Lonely? Would you want to enter into this image or do you feel some resistance to it?
- Jesus tells us to bring our burdens to him, that he will give us rest. Do you feel as if Jesus is truly able to carry your burdens? Or would you rather keep your burdens to yourself?
- In times of pain, suffering, and anxiety, do you put your total trust in Christ? Or would you rather handle things on your own than undergo the death of self depicted in the Four of Swords? Why?
- Reflect on the tomb in the Four of Swords. What feelings are brought up by that kind of surrender? Anxiety? Relief?

- In the upper-left-hand corner of this image, in the stained glass window, Jesus is blessing someone, a symbol of what we receive when we surrender our burdens to God. Have you ever felt this blessedness in response to surrender? If so, what did it feel like?
- How can you make this kind of surrender more foundational in your own life? Can you maybe start small, laying down one sword at a time, surrendering lesser things as a stepping stone to surrendering bigger things?

FIVE OF SWORDS

Put away from you all bitterness and wrath and anger
and wrangling and slander, together with all malice.
(Ephesians 4:31)

One of the most famous stories in the Bible is the story of Cain
and Abel. As the story goes, Cain and Abel are brothers; Cain is
a farmer and Abel is a shepherd. When these two brothers give
offerings to God, God prefers Abel's offerings of sheep to Cain's
offerings of grain. The Bible does not tell us why God prefers
Abel's offerings, and this mystery is one of the cruelties of suffering. Sometimes it seems that God favors others over us. Sometimes
our brother appears, for no reason at all, to have an easier life than
we ourselves have. Eaten up by this mystery and wholly unable
to bear his brother's good fortune, Cain viciously murders Abel.

Cain felt inferior to his brother, and his envy created a destructive force that rippled out from him, causing even more suffering. Instead of facing his woundedness with courage, he allowed it to fester and grow until it spilled out into violence. We see this same cruelty in the Five of Swords. A man holding three swords has won an obvious victory over the two people who walk away from him. Here is a man like Cain, a man who believes that he can only win if others lose, a man who sees his own woundedness as an excuse to wound others. He has hurt these people and he seems to have enjoyed it, but what has he gained in return?

As punishment, God condemns Cain to a life of wandering isolation. He becomes a homeless fugitive, separated from his family and his work and his native land. Cain's punishment is a lesson for Cain, but it is a lesson for us as well. When we refuse to face our own woundedness—when we refuse to own it—we instead thrust our woundedness onto others. In doing so, we cause needless suffering and we sever any connection we have with other people. This same isolating loneliness is present in the Five of Swords. Our victor stands in the foreground, looking smug with all his swords. The two people behind him are walking away from him, shoulders slumped and looking dejected. What has the victor won in this scenario? He is alone now; he has inherited the same isolation as Cain, separated from friendship and family. There is no real relationship between the people in this image. There is only a violent separateness born of one man's woundedness. Cain's story, and the Five of Swords, show us the cost of cruelty. When we see our own suffering as an excuse to cause more suffering, all we get in return is loneliness.

After Cain murders Abel, God confronts him, asking Cain where Abel has gone. Cain replies with those now-famous words, "I do not know; am I my brother's keeper?" (Genesis 4:9). What Cain is really saying here is that Abel is not his problem, so why the hell should he care? In answering a question with a question, Cain is attempting to absolve himself of responsibility. He sees only his own pain, and so no one else's pain matters. It is easy to imagine that the figure in the Five of Swords, with his cruel grin, would answer God's question in the same way. He obviously feels no responsibility toward the two people in the background. If he did, he would not treat them with such violence. We can choose the way of Cain and the way of the Five of Swords, cruel and distancing. We can choose to see our suffering as the only suffering that matters, casting aside responsibility for anyone else. We can also make a different choice, though. We can ask ourselves with true sincerity, "Am I my brother's keeper?" We can say yes, and we can watch the change in ourselves, from envy to acceptance and from resentment to love and from isolation to communion.

REFLECTIONS

- There are many verses in the Bible that speak against anger, including Proverbs 15:1 ("A soft answer turns away wrath, but a harsh word stirs up anger"), Proverbs 14:29 ("Whoever is slow to anger has great understanding"), and Psalm 37:8 ("Refrain from anger, and forsake wrath"). Reflect on these verses and others that you know. Do you see their lessons played out in the Five of Swords? If so, how?
- Which person in this image do you relate to more? Have there been times in your life when you have been the cruel victor? What about the two people suffering at the victor's hands? What did it feel like?

- Have you ever used your own suffering as an excuse to cause suffering for others? How did it make you feel?
- Cain's punishment for the murder of Abel was isolation. Have you ever, in your suffering, pushed other people away? If so, do you feel as if it eased your suffering? Why or why not?
- Reflect on Cain's famous question, "Am I my brother's keeper?" Who are your brothers? For whose keeping are you responsible?
- How might it change your life to spend more time focusing on the suffering of others rather than your own suffering? Might it make your own suffering easier to bear?

SIX OF SWORDS

Blessed be the God and Father of our Lord Jesus Christ, the Father of mercies and the God of all consolation, who consoles us in all our affliction, so that we may be able to console those who are in any affliction with the consolation with which we ourselves are consoled by God. (2 Corinthians 1:3–4)

In the Gospel of John, there is a story about Jesus and his friend Lazarus. Lazarus falls ill, and his sisters send word about it to Jesus. Jesus goes to them, but by the time he gets there, Lazarus has died. Jesus knows, and we know, that this story ends with Lazarus's resurrection from the dead. However, Jesus does not perform this miracle right away. He does not barrel in to "fix" the situation. He does not rush onto the scene with a hurried promise to make everything better. He does not instantly undo the sisters' grief, though he could. Instead, Jesus does something infinitely more loving. Jesus weeps with them. Even though he knows that his own divine miracle is a hair's breadth away, he first takes time to mourn with a grieving family. To be deeply present in another's suffering is a mercy unlike any other. This is true compassion. This is how we love each other in suffering, and this love is what we see played out in the Six of Swords. Two hunched figures sit in a boat, traveling down a river in a boat laden with swords. They are grieving, but they are not alone; a man steers their boat. There is sadness here, but there is no desolation.

When people we love are suffering, we want to make the suffering go away. Obviously, this is not always possible, and so it is easy to feel helpless in the face of sorrow. The story of Jesus and Lazarus's family is helpful inasmuch as it shows us what we *can* do. We cannot raise Lazarus from the dead, but we can weep with Lazarus's sisters. We can always offer presence, and this is no meager gift. In fact, it takes great courage. Look at the man in the Six of Swords. He is offering true compassionate presence to the woman and child. This man could have stayed on the safe shore. Instead, he has chosen to put himself in the same boat of pain as the woman and child. He has chosen not to flinch at another's agony. He has chosen to enter into another's darkest moment, knowing that he cannot fix it but only accompany it. These swords cannot be thrown overboard; they can only be carried along. While we cannot fix everyone's problems, this companionship in suffering is one of the many ways we can be Christ in the world. We can choose to stay where people suffer, and we can bear witness to love. We can make sure that when others suffer, they do not do so alone.

The Six of Swords shows us how to offer compassionate presence, but it also reminds us that sometimes we will be like the woman and child in this image, huddled together and sitting among a burden of grief we cannot escape without drowning. In our suffering, we will sometimes need to reach out to other people, to receive the compassion that people offer us, to allow them into our little boats of sorrow. In truth, this is often a much more difficult place for us, because it is a place of true helplessness. Extending compassion to another is sometimes easier than accepting compassion for ourselves. The Six of Swords reminds us, though, that compassion is a reciprocal act. It is a gift to help others carry their suffering, but it is also a gift to have people help us carry our own. To know that someone is accompanying us on the journey can make the journey easier. This is one of the great gifts of Christianity, this gentle reminder that, while we can give compassion, we can also receive it. We can love, and we can let ourselves be loved.

REFLECTIONS

- Spend some time reflecting on this image. Who do you relate to more? The man steering the boat? Or the woman and child? Why?
- Have you ever offered compassionate presence to someone in suffering? Do you feel like it helped? Why or why not?
- Have you ever been offered compassionate presence in your own suffering? If so, how did it make you feel?
- Reflect on the story of Jesus and Lazarus. What do you think it says about the importance of compassionate presence that Jesus offered it to Lazarus's sisters instead of rushing in to "fix" things?

- Do you feel more comfortable giving compassion or receiving it? Why?
- Spend some time with the idea that we can be Christ in the world by entering more fully into the suffering of others. Do you feel like you're good at that? Or do you resist it? Why?

SEVEN OF SWORDS

The wicked flee when no one pursues, but the righteous are as bold as a lion. (Proverbs 28:1)

A desire for safety is one of our most deeply rooted human instincts. No one ever wants to feel pain, and as a result we find ourselves constantly seeking security and comfort for ourselves. This instinct for self-preservation is not a bad thing. We have to survive, after all. That being said, the desire for safety—like any human desire—can be taken too far. Our instinct to seek security can be pushed to an intemperate extreme, can cause us to turn in on ourselves to an unhealthy degree. Our constant need for comfort can so easily warp into sin, and it happens when we consistently start to put our own needs above the needs of everyone else. Selfishness takes hold, and we stop looking out for others and start looking out only for ourselves. It is, like many sins, a case of blind ego. The Seven of Swords illustrates for us this sin, this craving for safety, which bends in on itself and becomes ugly and distorted. The intentions of this man are understandable. Like all of us, he wants to be safe. However, his actions are dishonorable. In order to save his own neck, he has stolen an armful of swords from his camp and has crept away, abandoning his comrades.

To be a coward is to be unwilling to feel pain for another. It is to see one's own comfort as more important than anyone else's comfort. The Seven of Swords shows us the consequences of this cowardice. The thief in this image has ensured his own safety. He holds in his arms five swords, which is an absurd number of swords. This man has more resources than any one person would ever need in order to defend himself, and his smug expression tells us that he feels no remorse about this. He has convinced himself that this underhandedness is okay, because he must look out for himself. We know better, though. We see this thief with his glut of swords, and we see him tiptoeing away, and we see him leaving his comrades with nothing. They stand in the background of the image, still on the battlefield. We do not know what will happen to them, but we can make an accurate guess. They will suffer more because of the thief's anxious desire to protect only himself, because of his unwillingness to stay and fight with his friends. This is cowardice. This is smallness of heart. This thief is unwilling to see past his own selfish desire for safety, a desire that is acted on at the cost of everyone around him.

We could be this man. We could be this thief, and we have to decide not to be, because cowardice is the poorest way to define one's life. It is shameful to seek safety at the expense of the safety of others. It is shameful to cause more suffering for others simply to ease one's own. We, as Christians, are called to something braver than this. We are called to share our resources. We are called to stay and fight with and for our neighbors, to support and protect them even if it means accepting a certain amount of discomfort or danger. Jesus never promises us safety. He never promises us security. We must be more courageous than the thief in the Seven of Swords. We must have more heart than this man does. We must see past our own small and petty will, and we must remember that we are united to something bigger than our own small and petty selves. Is it easy to live with this kind of courage? Of course not. But we are called to something more noble than ease.

REFLECTIONS

- We all have an instinctual desire for safety. Spend some time with this idea. Do you feel like you let that instinct rule your life to an intemperate degree? Why or why not?
- Have you ever been like the thief in the Seven of Swords, finding yourself amassing security at the expense of others' safety? If so, how did it affect your life and your relationships?
- Have you ever been like the other men in the Seven of Swords, on the receiving end of another's selfishness? If so, what did that feel like?
- As Christians, we are called to follow the will of God rather than our own wills. Do you think that means that we might sometimes need to set aside our own instincts for safety and security in order to help ease the suffering of others? How might that idea change your life?

- The word "courage" comes from the Latin word *cor*, meaning "heart." To have courage is to act from the heart. Have you ever thought about courage in this way, as an act of love? If not, how might it change your view of courage?
- As a Christian, do you feel specifically called to courage? How can you cultivate a spirit of courage in your own life?

EIGHT OF SWORDS

Naked I came from my mother's womb, and naked shall I return there; the Lord gave, and the Lord has taken away; blessed be the name of the Lord.
(Job 1:21)

One of the most beloved characters in the biblical tradition is Job. His story is familiar to most of us. Job is a righteous man, blessed by God. His life is rich and lovely, and then Satan enters the picture. Satan wants to test the limits of Job's piety, and God gives Satan permission to do so. Satan proceeds to strip every good thing from Job's life: his family, his livelihood, his health. Job is reduced to misery, and like anyone who experiences loss, he wants to know why. He spends much of his biblical story lamenting his misfortune and demanding that God tell him why this is happening to him, what he has done to deserve such suffering, why he was even born if this is what life is like. Job is a man trapped and blinded by suffering. He has had everything taken from him and feels wholly immobilized by the painful mystery of it. The Eight of Swords is tarot's representation of this suffocating feeling of loss. This is what it felt like for Job, and this is what it feels like for us. To be present in the Eight of Swords is to feel trapped by the mystery of suffering: wrapped up, blindfolded, caged by swords, separated from one's home and family, wholly alone.

Job demands answers from God, and eventually God comes onto the scene. Speaking from a dramatic whirlwind, God asks Job, "Where were you when I laid the foundation of the earth?" (Job 38:4). What a question! In a long monologue, God contrasts Job's weakness with God's omnipotence. God speaks for a very long time, and God does not answer a single one of Job's questions. God never tells Job why he is suffering. Instead, God reminds Job that this mystery of suffering is just that—a mystery. God offers Job a dramatic shift in perspective, and Job takes it. He stops fighting his inevitable suffering. He confesses God's power and his own lack of knowledge. He gives up his vain fight for answers to a problem he will never understand. While Job never learns the meaning of suffering, he learns something even better. He learns to live in the space of nonanswer. He learns to lean deeply into the mystery of it. This is the same radical shift in perspective into which the Eight of Swords invites us. This is an image from which we would like to escape, but what if we didn't? We want to fight our way out of suffering by demanding answers, but what if we surrendered to the mystery instead?

At first glance, the Eight of Swords seems to be a difficult image. If we look closely, however, we see that the woman here who is bound by cloth and trapped by swords is smiling. It is a small and secret Mona Lisa smile, but it is a smile nonetheless. The Eight of Swords is a scenario that begs for escape, and to ask ourselves to stay in this place goes against our human instincts for comfort and safety, but this woman has done so, and she has learned a secret, just as Job did. She has learned that if we are humble enough to open ourselves to the mystery of suffering, the mystery will open itself to us. If we surrender, we will be blessed beyond measure. Not with answers—nothing in life is that easy—but with something infinitely better. We will find faith, just as Job did. This is the secret of the Eight of Swords. In the Bible, it is those who are blind—those who do not see and still believe—who receive their sight. The woman in the Eight of Swords, like Job, is surrounded by suffering. Despite all that, she smiles, because the Lord can give and the Lord can take away, but the name of the Lord is always blessed. This is faith, and it is a gift. It is less satisfying than answers, but it is infinitely more beautiful.

REFLECTIONS

- Spend some time with the image of the Eight of Swords. What are your first reactions to it? Does it make you feel anxious? Curious? Sympathetic?
- Have you ever been in a situation like Job's, where you were suffering and demanding answers from God? Do you feel as if God answered your questions? If not, how did that feel?
- Humanity is haunted by the question of why bad things happen to good people. The Eight of Swords tells us, essentially, that we should stop trying to know. How does that feel for you?

- Reflect on what it might feel like to sink deeply into the space of the Eight of Swords rather than struggling to escape it. Does it feel good? Scary? Both?
- Do you feel closer to God in wrestling for answers or in surrendering to mystery? Why or why not? (There are no right or wrong answers to this question. Some of us are naturally more inclined to wrestle, some to surrender.)
- Reflect on the idea that our faith in God's goodness can be a different kind of answer to the question of suffering. How does that feel?

NINE OF SWORDS

I am weary with my moaning; every night I flood my
bed with tears; I drench my couch with my weeping.
(Psalm 6:6)

As Christians, we are taught to turn to God in our suffering. It is
a deep and unalterable truth that God loves us, and that God is always present to us in our pain. This truth does not always feel like
truth, though. Sometimes, we cry out to God in the darkness that
we are afraid and that our suffering feels like too much to bear,
and instead of feeling the loving presence of God, we feel only the
terrifying lack of it. We turn to God, and it seems like God is not
there. This is not an unfamiliar feeling among people of faith. In
the book of Ruth, Naomi proclaims that "the hand of the Lord
has turned against me" (Ruth 1:13). In the Psalms, David begs to

know, "How long, O Lord? Will you forget me forever?" (Psalm 13:1). Even Christ felt abandoned during his earthly life, crying out on the cross, "My God, my God, why have you forsaken me?" (Matthew 27:46). Though this feeling might be familiar, it is no less terrifying for that, and tarot's Nine of Swords shows us the full force of that seeming abandonment. A man sits up in his bed, hunched over by the weight of this desolation. This is the dark night of the soul of which the mystics speak, and it feels like nothing less than true desertion.

When we feel as if God has abandoned us, the natural response is fear, and we see plenty of fear in the Nine of Swords. Behind the man in this image, we see nine swords stacked on the wall. They take up most of the image. Their hilts seem to be woven together as if every sword builds on another, and they all point to an unknown yet seemingly inconsolable future. The great temptation of the Nine of Swords is to believe in this inconsolable future. It is to believe that what we feel is reality, and this is an easy temptation, because the fear feels so very real. In the dark night of the soul—in the space of the Nine of Swords—it is easy to believe that God, for some unknown reason, no longer loves us. It is easy to believe that God has specifically rejected us. It is easy to believe that God is gone, lost to us forever. In these moments, God feels far away and hidden and ineffective, and the temptation is to believe that God is all of those things, instead of assuming that we might be wrong. To give fear this kind of leverage in our lives is to sink into despair. It is to fall asleep instead of daring to hope.

The Nine of Swords is a terrifying image, because the dark night of the soul is a terrifying ordeal. This image also shows us what to do, though, and it is simple. Stay awake. The man in the Nine of Swords is sitting up in bed and he is weeping. He is afraid, but he is not asleep. He is distressed, but he is not despairing. This dark night is not the place for despair. This is not the place where we give up. This is the place where we stay awake through the night, where we keep crying out even when it feels to us as if God is not there. This is a thing that is easy to say and much more difficult to actually do, because the terrible moment of the Nine of Swords is also the terrible moment when real faith comes into play. Here is the place where we must decide that God is near, whether we feel that God is near or not. In this way, the Nine of Swords invites us into the deepest interior submission, a letting go of what we may feel in order to grasp what we must believe. God is with us even here, and we are saved in this terrible darkness only by his tender mercy.

REFLECTIONS

- Have you ever had a moment in your life when you felt as if God had abandoned you? What was that like for you?
- Reflect on the idea that even Christ on the cross felt abandoned by God. How might that make feelings of desolation easier to bear?
- In the Nine of Swords, the swords are a representation of primal fears: that we are unlovable, that we are essentially alone, that life is meaningless. What fears do you see in the Nine of Swords? What if you could hand those fears to God in perfect trust?
- Reflect on the closely connected feelings of distress and despair. Have you ever tried to untangle the differences between the two? What do you think those differences are?

- In many ways, the Nine of Swords is about having faith even when your feelings tell you that you shouldn't. How might the idea that feelings are not necessarily fact change your relationship with faith?
- What practices can you cultivate in your life that might help you stay awake to God's mercy during times when mercy seems far away?

TEN OF SWORDS

Blessed are those who are persecuted for righteousness' sake, for theirs is the kingdom of heaven. (Matthew 5:10)

Christianity is a religion of shocking and scandalous love. We believe that God was made man to prove his love. We believe that Christ on earth was willing to love us even unto a humiliating death on a cross. We believe in a God who made a perfect sacrifice of his very self. This sacrifice is the bedrock of our faith. For God so loved the world that he gave us his life, and our religion is filled with saints who loved God enough to do the same. Christianity is also a religion of martyrs, and the Ten of Swords gives us an image of martyrdom. A man lies cruciform on the ground. Ten swords jut upward from his back, looking like so many crosses on a hill. It is not an easy image to look at, but it is a reminder that Christianity is not an easy religion. We are called to bear witness to Christ's love, and to be a martyr is to bear witness even unto death. The Ten of Swords, like the faith of the martyrs, asks us if we are willing to do the same. Are we willing to risk death for Christ as Christ risked death for us? How much are we willing to give? How far are we willing to go?

Martyrdom is not as common as it once was, and anyone reading these words is unlikely to ever face physical death for Christ. However, we are still called to accept the spiritual rationale behind the concept of martyrdom. In the Gospel of Matthew, Jesus tells his disciples, "If any want to become my followers, let them deny themselves and take up their cross and follow me" (Matthew 16:24). While we likely will never wind up nailed to a cross, we still have crosses to carry. Each one of us is specifically called to pick up a cross, and to pick up a cross is to be willing to die. It is to live with the weighty spirit of a martyr, loving Christ so fiercely that we would follow Christ anywhere, even to death. It is to exist in the place where we are bravely willing to suffer as Christ suffered, the place where every breath of our lives belongs to God. To live under the weight of a cross is to live in complete and utter surrender, because it is impossible to carry a heavy cross and also carry anything else.

The Ten of Swords shows us an image of a brutal martyrdom, but there is a noticeable lack of despair. There is death here, but there is no fear. In fact, the image is infused with a distinctive sense of hope, as if the darkness of this image were wrapped in light. In the background of the image is a new dawn breaking, a golden sky behind the black clouds. The martyr's face is turned to the rising sun, and his hand is making a traditional sign of divine blessing. While the Ten of Swords shows us the violence of martyrdom, it also shows us the strange and paradoxical blessedness of it. To live with the spirit of the martyrs is to live entirely without fear. Here is the place where there are no fears of suffering, of loss, or about the future. Everything is abandoned to God, and so nothing holds us back from God. Even the suffering becomes a blessing that draws us close to Christ's own loving sacrifice. This is what it means to be a martyr. If we truly pick up our crosses, we will find union with God. If we die to Christ, we will gain everything. Blessed are the hurting, for heaven is theirs.

REFLECTIONS

- What is your relationship with the concept of martyrdom? Does it carry positive or negative associations for you? Why?
- Do you think of Christianity as a religion of martyrdom? Do you feel as if we, as Christians, are called to a sort of spiritual martyrdom? Why or why not?
- Reflect on the idea that we all have crosses we are meant to pick up and carry with us. What is your cross? And how do you carry it?
- The Ten of Swords is an image of deep surrender. Spend some time with this idea of complete self-surrender to God. How does it feel?
- The Ten of Swords shows us that the natural end of loving as Christ loves is to die as Christ died. How can you bring into your own life that spirit of willingness to love at any cost? What would it take for you to do so?

- We live in a culture that encourages us to avoid suffering at all costs, so it can seem strange for us to think of suffering as a blessing. How might it change your conception of suffering to think about it as a way to become closer to God?

ACE OF CUPS

Those who drink of the water that I will give them will never be thirsty. The water that I will give will become in them a spring of water gushing up to eternal life. (John 4:14)

On the night before his crucifixion, Jesus held a Passover meal with his disciples. During this meal, Jesus took a loaf of bread, blessed it, and passed it around, saying "Take, eat; this is my body" (Matthew 26:26). He did the same with the wine, saying, "Drink from it, all of you; for this is my blood of the covenant, which is poured out for many for the forgiveness of sins" (Matthew 26:27–28). This utterly sacred moment marked the institution of the Eucharist, the great sacrament of divine love.

What Jesus offered to his disciples during the Last Supper was more than food and drink. What Jesus freely offered them, in the form of bread and wine, was his very self. In the sacrament of the Eucharist, this loving sacrifice echoes through eternity, continuing to nourish us. The Eucharist is love itself, poured out for many. And the Ace of Cups, in all its eucharistic glory, is tarot's representation of this deeply nourishing love. In this profoundly mystical image, a dove descends with the host above a chalice overflowing with five streams, which represent Christ's wounds. This is nothing less than the wellspring of divine love. It is the love that it is in God's very nature to give, and it is given for us and to us.

Such deep spiritual nourishment is an invitation to admit that we need to be spiritually nourished. Such grace prompts us to reconcile ourselves to the ways in which we need that grace. In order to drink from this cup, we must first admit that we are thirsty. In Psalm 63:1, the psalmist cries out, "O God, you are my God, I seek you, my soul thirsts for you; my flesh faints for you, as in a dry and weary land where there is no water." We long for this love. We thirst for it. We need it as we need water, as we need food, as we need sunshine and fresh air and a place to lay our heads at night. The need for this grace is an intrinsic part of who we are. It is in Christ's nature to pour out this love for us, and it is in our nature to need it. We are made to want this.

The Ace of Cups emerges from a cloud like the supernatural blessing that it is, begging us to drink. It is easy to look at this image—at this blessing—and think, who would refuse this? It is the purest peace. It is the unending and eternal grace. It is the love from which all love flows. We can turn away from it, though, if we want to. We do have a choice. While it is in God's nature to give us this deeply nourishing love, and while it is in our nature to want it, a gift is only a gift if one has a choice about whether or not to accept it. Christ loves us, and Christ wants to give us the love for which we are made, but Christ does not force his love on us, because a love freely given must also be freely received. This love—this relentless affection—is always available for us, and we must choose to accept it. We must choose to let our own cups be filled with this wellspring of life. We must not turn away, but instead accept this invitation to be open and receptive to the love for which we are made. If we do, we will never be thirsty again.

REFLECTIONS

- The Ace of Cups is an obvious nod to the Eucharist. Reflect on your relationship with the Eucharist or with the idea of communion. Do you feel the love of God in this sacrament? Why or why not?
- The word "Eucharist" comes from the Greek *eukharistia,* meaning "grateful." Does the image of the Ace of Cups inspire a posture of gratitude for you? Why or why not?
- The Ace of Cups is a tender reminder that God loves us deeply. Does it feel natural to assume God's specific love for you? Or does the personal nature of it feel strange? Why?
- Have you ever felt the spiritual thirst to which the Ace of Cups alludes? If so, how did you satisfy that thirst?

- Reflect on the idea that God does not force his love on us, that it is a thing we can choose to accept. Do you feel comfortable accepting God's love? Or do you feel an impulse to reject it? Why?
- How do you think your life might change if you accepted the gift of the Ace of Cups?

TWO OF CUPS

Beloved, let us love one another, because love is from God; everyone who loves is born of God and knows God. (1 John 4:7)

In the beginning of time, God created not one person but two. Adam could not have lived alone in the garden of Eden any more than Adam could have lived without food to eat or water to drink or the feeling of sunshine on his face. Such a perfect and grace-filled life needed another perfect and grace-filled life with which to share it, and so God made Eve as well. This longing for companionship is a vital function of who we are. It is a God-given gift, one that has been present with us since the very beginning. From the first lines of our story, we have craved connection with one another. We want to reach out to another, to touch and be touched, to be in union. Created in the image of God, who is himself love, we are made to love and to be loved. The Two of Cups is a beautiful representation of this instinctual desire for union with each other, the need to feel connected. Two people meet, hands touching, offering their cups. This is a relationship of love. Perhaps it is marriage, perhaps it is friendship, perhaps it is companionship. Love takes many forms, after all. But whatever form it takes, real love is always a movement toward another, a desire to share a life.

The Two of Cups shows us an ideal of the love for which we are made. The two people in this image are exchanging cups. They are reaching out for each other in mutual desire. This is not an image of one person giving a cup and one person taking. This is not an image of one person holding power while another submits to it. This is not a union where one person is being vulnerable and one person is not, for that would not be a union at all. This is a flow of love willingly exchanged. It is a relationship of perfect balance, where each person opens themselves to the other with great trust and tenderly receives what is offered with great respect. It is a reminder that to love truly is to drink from someone's cup, and also to let the other person drink from yours. Such a love cannot happen from a place of self-protection or power. A true connection such as we see in the Two of Cups takes an astonishing amount of vulnerability, because a true connection is nothing less than the mutual giving of the deepest self. Such a perfect love as we see in the Two of Cups can feel rare—we are, after all, only human— but it is a love we should strive for all the same. This is a true relationship, and it is in this relationship that we find the divine.

Above the couple in this image is both a caduceus and a winged lion, respective symbols of divine healing and divine power. With these symbols, the Two of Cups reminds us of the ways in which human love and divine love are intimately connected. Our ability to be in true connection with one another is a gift from God, and this gift was given because human love is where we learn about divine love. We learn how to be open with God by first being open with each other. We learn vulnerability with God by practicing vulnerability with each other. Indeed, it would be nearly impossible for us to understand the divine love of God without the template of generous and tender and vulnerable human love. In a mysterious way, all authentic human love is also divine love, because it is in this intimate communion that we encounter God. In their deep love for each other, the couple in the Two of Cups points to a love bigger than themselves. When we can also love in this way—with deep respect and mutual vulnerability—we become people who reveal divine love to each other. When we love in this way, we echo God's love for us. When we love in this way, we know God.

REFLECTIONS

- The Two of Cups teaches us about the ways we see divine love in our human relationships. Do you feel like your relationships with other people are a way to know God more fully? Why or why not?
- Have you experienced the intimate communion of the Two of Cups? If so, with whom? And how did it feel for you?
- Do you feel as if divine love is present in your truest, deepest relationships with people? Do you feel as if that love echoes a divine love? Why or why not?
- Do you feel comfortable loving people in such an open way? Or does it feel unsafe? Why?

- What are some ways in which you can cultivate more open and loving relationships like this in your own life? How can you practice that sort of generosity?
- Do you feel comfortable in relationships of mutual giving like the one in the Two of Cups? Or do you feel safer or more comfortable or more protected in a relationship in which you are the sole giver or the sole receiver? Why?

THREE OF CUPS

O come, let us sing to the Lord; let us make a joyful
noise to the rock of our salvation! (Psalm 95:1)

In the book of Exodus, when Pharaoh's men are drowned in the
Red Sea after the Israelites cross safely through the parted waters,
Miriam and her women dance and sing in exaltation. In 2 Samuel, when the Ark of the Covenant is brought to Jerusalem, David
dances in jubilation. In the Gospel of Luke, when the prodigal son
returns home after many lonely years, his father joyfully welcomes
him home with open arms and throws him a lavish party. The
Bible is filled with stories like this. They are stories of honoring
God with dancing and singing, stories of gladness in the presence
of the Lord, stories of love poured out in joyful celebration. These
stories remind us that we are meant to be people of joy. When we

feel the presence of God's care, we want to dance about it. When we touch upon deep contentment, we want to celebrate it. The Three of Cups shows us this instinct for celebration. Three women dance in a circle, cups raised in a toast. They move with light steps, blushing and smiling, flowers in their hair, surrounded by an abundant harvest. God always loves us, and so there is always cause to raise a glass.

This sense of joyful, abundant celebration we see in the Three of Cups infuses our entire religion. Christianity is all about the art of celebration. Across the liturgical year are scattered solemnities such as Easter, Christmas, Pentecost, and Epiphany, chances to dance and drink and dine. On any given day there is a saint whose feast day we can celebrate. Every week we remember the Sabbath and keep it holy. To live deeply within Christianity is to mark time by feast days. It is to live always in either celebration or anticipation of one, and we are able to live this way because our whole religion is built on the ever-merciful love of God, the cup that is eternally poured out for us and for the forgiveness of our sins. This is true festivity. It is true festivity because it is a response to something outside of ourselves, a response to a reality we encounter in the love of Christ. A true Christian celebration is more than just a party. It is an instinctual response to living with open eyes in a good world made by a loving God.

This culture of deep festivity draws us to each other, and we see this communion in the Three of Cups. The women in the Three of Cups do not dance separately but together. Forming an intimate circle, they gladly raise their cups to heaven, toasting God in love and toasting each other in friendship. This is the nature of joy. It prompts us to share it with others. The culture of joyful Christian celebration draws us together. True festivity gathers us in, reminding us that we do not dance alone but together. We do not sing in somber solo refrain but raise our voices as one. We do not feast at empty tables because we are all invited to the feast. The dance we see in the Three of Cups is not an exclusive affair. We are all loved by God, and so we all have a part in this celebration. We all belong here. We all get to take part in this joy. This is the deep communion of Christian life, drawn together in the dance and raising a glass for the God who gives us love and life and eternal mercy.

REFLECTIONS

- Spend some time reflecting on stories of joy and celebration in the Bible. Do they feel more prominent in your mind than stories of struggle and sorrow? Why or why not?

- Do you think of Christianity as a religion of festivity? Why or why not?

- What are your favorite ways to celebrate joys in your life? Can you celebrate the joys of faith in those same ways? Eating, drinking, dancing, singing?

- Do you follow the liturgical year? If so, do you feel like it adds true celebration to your life?

- The Three of Cups is an image of communal celebration. Whom do you celebrate with? Who are your partners in festivity?

- How can you foster a deeper sense of festivity in your own life? How can you make more room for celebration?

FOUR OF CUPS

Restore to me the joy of your salvation, and sustain in
me a willing spirit. (Psalm 51:12)

We all have within us an instinctual thirst for divine love, a longing for grace. Jesus offers us this gift of infinite mercy, and it seems
like it should be easy to accept it, right? The spiritual life is never
so easy, though, and sometimes a curious thing happens when
confronted with this divine love. Sometimes we are offered the
cup, and instead of feeling what one would expect to feel—joy,
gladness, acceptance—we feel precisely nothing. At the moment
when we should expect to feel thirst, we feel only a distinct lack of
it. We are given the chance at God's love, and all we feel is boredom. Sometimes our hearts do not treasure what they should, and
the Four of Cups shows us this indifferent, lukewarm response to

God's love. The proffered cup in the Four of Cups is an allusion to the Ace of Cups, emerging out of a cloud. The man sitting under the tree is not impressed, however. He has his arms crossed in a slumped posture of defensiveness. He gazes downward, not at the divine cup of blessing but at the three ordinary cups on the ground in front of him. This is what it looks like to be unmoved by God's love, to be unable to muster any response beyond a spiritual shrug.

The desert fathers of early Christianity had a particular word for this feeling. They called it acedia, which translates directly from the Latin derivative as "lack of care." Defined by the desert fathers, acedia is a lack of appetite for those things for which the soul hungers. It can be seen as a sort of spiritual sluggishness. That sluggishness is suggested by the man's posture in the Four of Cups, sitting cross-legged under a tree with his head hanging and his eyes closed in the heat of the day. He is weary and listless and wholly unable to gather the energy needed to act on God's love. He is also alone, and this solitude is another distinct aspect of acedia. It is the nature of acedia to cause one to wish to be by oneself, to remain undisturbed by the presence of God, to be unbothered by the effort of extending a hand to take the cup. When acedia grips us, we want to be left alone more than we want the presence of God. We simply cannot bring ourselves to care about anything in particular. In these feelings of sluggishness and seclusion, acedia keeps us small. It keeps us bored. It keeps us sitting under a tree with our arms crossed like a petulant child.

The spiritual apathy we see in the Four of Cups is a frustrating but not unusual problem in the Christian life. "Acedia" is not a common word these days, but it is a common struggle, and this listlessness can affect even those well-intentioned. The Four of Cups does not offer a solution, really, but it does offer grace. It names the struggle and forgives it in the same moment. This cup which is so gently given is always available to us. God could withdraw this cup, but he does not. The offer always stands; the cup never leaves. Our love may waver, but God's love never does. This man sits under his tree with his arms crossed, and he is welcome to do so as long as he would like. We are imperfect, and we will struggle with things we should be able to do with ease, but the Four of Cups reminds us that there is no rush. We will not be punished for this struggle. We will not be damned for needing time. God is ever-merciful, and God will wait, and God will be ready to rejoice when we decide we are ready to embrace the cup with an open hand.

REFLECTIONS

- Spend some time with the man in this image. Can you relate to his feelings of boredom and sluggishness? Does your spiritual life ever feel this way to you? If so, describe what those feelings are like for you.
- Psalm 51:12 encourages us to pray for the restoration of joy. If you've ever felt the way the man in the Four of Cups feels, did you consider praying in this way? How might that help?
- Have you ever heard of acedia? Is it something that you recognize in your own life or in the lives of people you know? If so, how does it show itself?
- Have you ever felt a desire to be away from God? To be unbothered by God? To be alone as the man in the Four of Cups is alone? If so, how did that feel?

- What are some practices you can put into place in your spiritual life that might help you keep a willing spirit toward God?
- There is a gentle patience that is present in the Four of Cups. How might an understanding of that divine patience affect your spiritual life?

FIVE OF CUPS

Repent therefore, and turn to God so that your sins may be wiped out. (Acts 3:19)

Christianity is a religion that holds its believers to an impossibly high standard. We are expected to love as Christ loves, and no one lives up to that expectation. In ways both big and small, we are constantly failing to be our best selves. We do things we should not do. We do not do things we should do. We act in selfish smallness. In short, we sin, and the problem with sin is that it feels good until it doesn't. One day we look up and realize how far we have strayed, and the Five of Cups shows us this recognition. It shows us the wave of regret, the moment in which we realize the ways in which we have fallen short of what we should be. In this image, a man stands alone, wearing black, head hung low. He gazes at three cups in front of him. They are overturned, spilled and impossible to unspill. This is a picture of deep regret, but regret is not the end of the story. While the Five of Cups is an image of mourning, it is also an image of hope. Christianity might hold us to an impossible standard, but Christianity also offers us an impossible mercy.

We are prone to fail ourselves and others in myriad ways, and that sense of regret is palpable in this image, but we are not doomed to eternal sadness. The man in black mourns his overturned cups, but in this image are also two cups that stand upright. They are right behind him, so close that if he turned around he would brush them with his cloak. These cups are new cups. They are full cups of divine blessing, unspilled and unbroken, and they are always available to us when we are ready to receive them. These cups remind us that while there are a million ways for us to make mistakes, there is no mistake that God cannot forgive. There are not three cups here to match the three spilled cups, because while God will certainly forgive every mistake, he is not a genie who will undo the consequences of every mistake we make. There is a persistent sadness in the Five of Cups: we may still bear the hurt of our sins. However, these two cups still invite us to healing. Mercy is ever present, and God is always ready to offer us a cup full of blessing. It is the very nature of God to be always waiting for us, the eternal Father of interminably prodigal children. We can and will knock over cups and make a mess of things, but forgiveness is never more than a step away.

It sometimes feels easier to brood on sin than to enter into a life more holy, but the Five of Cups shows us the simplicity and gift of it. It shows us how simple it can be. This man in black is so close to God's love, close enough to reach out and touch it. All he has to do is admit that he wants it, that he wants love more than sin. That's it. There is no trick to receiving God's mercy. The man must simply be willing to turn around. He must be willing to let go of his mess of regrets, to leave behind the overturned cups. Once he does, he can follow the path marked by the new cups. He can cross the bridge into a new and better life. God wants to be known and God is always present to us, and, truly, all we have to do is turn around. If we come to God with our hurts—if we approach God with true regret in our hearts—we will be forgiven. We can take the cup of blessing and enter into a new life. We can move away from bitterness and remorse and we can take the first steps in remembering our union with God.

REFLECTIONS

- Reflect on the idea that Christianity is a faith of impossible standards, that we are bound to make mistakes in living up to our call to love as Christ loves. How does that feel for you?
- The three overturned cups in this image symbolize regret. What might the three cups represent for you, specifically?
- The Five of Cups can be seen as an image that prompts us to metanoia. In the New Testament, metanoia is often translated as "repentance," but the fuller meaning of the word involves a changing of mind or a change of direction. How might it change your ideas on repentance to see it as a turning toward God?
- Do you ever feel as if you hold on to your regrets and past mistakes? Do you find it difficult to turn away from them? Why or why not?

- The Five of Cups shows us the ways in which God can forgive us without necessarily correcting our mistakes. Can you believe that God is merciful and also that we are still held responsible for the consequences of our actions? If so, how might that feel for you?
- Reflect on a time when you felt truly forgiven by God. How did it change you?

SIX OF CUPS

But to all who received him, who believed in his name,
he gave power to become children of God. (John 1:12)

In the Gospel of Matthew, there is a story in which the disciples come to Jesus and ask him about the greatest person in heaven. The disciples want to know who it is because they also want to be great. They want prestige and honor, authority and influence. God himself comes to earth and ushers in a new age, and from its very dawn, men want to know how to claim power in it. In response to the disciples' question, Jesus calls a child to him. And then he tells the disciples, "Truly I tell you, unless you change and become like children, you will never enter the kingdom of heaven. Whoever becomes humble like this child is the greatest in the kingdom of heaven" (Matthew 18:3–4). The disciples wanted greatness, and

Jesus gave them a child. In this conversation, the disciples were reminded that, in the kingdom of heaven, true greatness lies not in worldly power and prestige but in the precise opposite. We become great by becoming like little children, and the Six of Cups is tarot's representation of this Christian teaching. An image of simple sweetness, it shows us what it looks like in practice to move through the world in the childlike way in which we have been instructed.

The Six of Cups gives us a startling, uncomplicated image of love. One child offers another child a cup with a flower in it. It is a simple gesture of affection, sweet and plain and completely free from irony or arch distance. The child in the Six of Cups does not ask whether or not the friend deserves the flower, or whether the flower is enough or not enough. There is nothing to prove and nothing to gain from this gesture of love. With this achingly earnest act of kindness, the child simply gives what is available to be given. And there is much available; the scene is filled with flowers. There is no sense of scarcity here, because children do not love in a miserly way. They do not think of love as a finite resource to be hoarded, but as something meant to be shared. Behind the children, a sentry walks away. His distance from the rest of the scene reminds us of the unguardedness of the children's love. Standing in the middle of the town square, surrounded by abundance, they feel safe and secure. They know that they are cared for, and so they can care for each other in turn.

As adults, to love in such a simple and humble way can actually be quite difficult. Many of us are so engrossed in worry about our own security that being like a child can feel counterintuitive. We look at a scene like this and think that it is too simple or too trite, that there must be some catch or a joke that we're missing. We are used to adult relationships, which are much more likely to be transactional, built on scarcity and scorekeeping. Jesus gave us an image of a child in the kingdom of heaven because the child sees the world as God wants us to see it. To love in such an openhearted way as an adult can make us feel foolish or naive, but we must allow ourselves to feel that way. There is a directness about these two children that we, as adults, need to relearn. We are meant to give and receive love in simple and generous ways. We are meant to practice charity, and nothing is less complicated, in truth. To be childishly charitable is to be unguarded and earnest and more concerned with kindness than with power. It is to love with open hearts and full trust, even when it feels silly, because the more we love like children, the more we love like God.

REFLECTIONS

- Reflect on the story from the Gospel of Matthew. Do you relate to the disciples who were eager to know about greatness in heaven? Why or why not?
- We live in a culture that prizes power and prestige. What might it feel like for you to prioritize being childlike over being powerful? To seek love rather than influence?
- Spend some time with the Six of Cups. Do you feel as if you love in the way described in this image? Do you feel as if you receive this kind of love? If so, what does it feel like?
- Have you spent much time around children? If so, have you noticed the openness with which they give and receive affection? Do you feel as if you could love in that way? Why or why not?

- The Six of Cups reminds us that love is meant to be given away. Do you think about love in this way? Or do you think of it as something to safeguard? Why?
- To love as a child loves is to move through the world with more naivety than we are perhaps used to as adults. What would it feel like for you to perhaps be perceived as naive by other adults?

SEVEN OF CUPS

Do not be deceived, my beloved. (James 1:16)

We are creatures of desire. Restlessly discontent, we are always seeking the elusive something that will bring us satisfaction. Always we could be happier. Always our lives could be better. Always there is room for more. Our lives are defined by the things we want, and the world in which we live offers us no shortage of answers to that want. Our culture is always trying to sell us something, always twisting our desire to its advantage, always offering up things that promise pleasure or power or praise. The Seven of Cups gives us an image of this overwhelming, fever-pitched temptation, an image of all the things that try to pull at our attention, an image of beguiling promise. A man stands before seven cups filled with symbols representing seven glittering temptations. A dragon encourages greedy hoarding of wealth. A castle promises security and safety at the expense of keeping others out. A laurel wreath, resting atop a poisoned cup, beckons us with fame. A shrouded, glowing figure invites us into a deifying of the self. Every one of these cups is filled with something bright and alluring. Will these things bring us the contentment we so crave? Or, in choosing this vision, are we trying to satisfy our infinite desire with things that only exacerbate that desire?

The Seven of Cups is designed to be beguiling. Who would not want the beauty suggested by the woman's face? Who would not want the cleverness of the snake? Who would not be drawn in by a pile of gleaming jewels? We can understand why the man in this image has been taken in by this vision. He looks at all these shimmering temptations and does not see the vanity of fame or the greed of wealth or the cruelty of cleverness. He only sees a vast freedom without limits. His arms are open to it, as if he can hardly believe his luck, as if he cannot decide which lovely cup to take first. There is a sinister undertone to the Seven of Cups, though. The man seems to be literally overtaken by this vision. We hardly notice him compared to the cups; he is nothing but a shadow, eclipsed by the glimmering fantasy. His barely there presence is a reminder of the ways in which it is possible to give too much of ourselves to worldly desire. When we focus on these temptations—when we let ourselves fall prey to them—we lose ourselves. When we let ourselves be led into the illusory promise of worldly contentment, we run the risk of being unable to escape it.

We want what the Seven of Cups claims to offer, and sometimes our want can trick us into assigning value to that which has none. These seven cups are presented to us as reality, but this is nothing more than a vision. The dream of the Seven of Cups is just that—a dream. These cups, which look so lovely, are merely tempting mirages, lacking any substance or meaning. Not one of these cups will bring us lasting happiness. Not one of these cups will satisfy the deepest desire for which we are made. We are made for something more real than the smoke and mirrors of the Seven of Cups. What we hunger for is the infinite, and not a single finite thing offered in this vision will satisfy that hunger. We are made for real love, not a fantasy. If we see the Seven of Cups for what it is, it will serve as a reminder of the many things in and of the world that promise us the kind of contentment that only God can give. We must have strength to remember what it is we should be seeking, to resist losing ourselves to glimmering illusion.

REFLECTIONS

- Spend some time thinking about the things the world tells you that you need. What do you *really* need?
- What are some ways in which you can push back against the kind of fevered stimulation we see in the Seven of Cups?
- Reflect on the different temptations present in the Seven of Cups. Which of these feels the most tempting for you? Why?
- Have you ever had an experience of losing yourself to a desire that did not satisfy? Have you ever felt like the figure in the Seven of Cups? What did that feel like for you?

- The Seven of Cups is only an illusion. How can you remind yourself of this? How can you remember what you are truly made for?
- How might it change your perspective on desire to remember that you are made to love and be loved by God? Might it make these temptations easier to resist?

EIGHT OF CUPS

When you search for me, you will find me; if you seek
me with all your heart. (Jeremiah 29:13)

The Gospels tell us a little story about Peter and Andrew, two of
the disciples. Peter and Andrew are fishing on the sea of Galilee
one day, and Jesus is walking along the beach. Jesus sees them,
and he calls out that they should follow him. With startling speed,
Peter and Andrew heed that call, dropping everything to follow
Jesus. Only a few verses long, this story is easy to miss, but it contains one of the great mysteries of our faith. The call of Jesus is one
that many of us know. It is the still voice that speaks to our interior restlessness for God, beckoning us to leave the old life behind
and seek something deeper. The Eight of Cups offers us another
example of the heeding of this call. In it, a man walks away from

eight cups. There is nothing wrong with the eight cups he has; they are all intact and upright and carefully stacked. A cup is missing, though, and it is obvious. The gap is noticeable. Though the man's life is perfectly fine, something is not quite right. The man is off on a journey to find the missing cup. He has paid attention to his own interior restlessness and he is letting it lead him. He is answering the divine call.

This seeking can feel uncomfortable and dangerous, because it requires that we leave behind the familiar. When Peter and Andrew were called by Christ, they did not take their fishing nets with them. They dropped them, leaving behind their entire livelihoods. The pilgrim in the Eight of Cups has done the same. He has left behind his carefully stacked cups, taking nothing with him on his journey except his walking stick and the clothes on his back. There is comfort in the eight carefully stacked cups, and to leave them behind does not always feel good. Like this pilgrim, though, we must leave behind everything we know. We must walk into the night of God's mystery with nothing. The Eight of Cups reminds us that in order to seek the mysterious and ultimately unknowable love of God, we must detach ourselves from the comfortably familiar, and this detachment will sometimes feel like being led into a wild landscape. We will sometimes feel like we are wandering around in the dark without anything to guide us, without our usual sources of comfort and meaning. We might think we are lost, because we do not understand, but that is okay. We are allowed to not understand.

There is a moon in the Eight of Cups, a moon with a gentle face. It calls to mind the mysterious and enigmatic Moon archetype of the major arcana, and it reminds us that the mystery is the point. To be present in the Eight of Cups is to seek the love of God above all else, and in order to do that, we must be willing to stumble around in the dark. Indeed, "stumbling around in the dark" can also be called "faith." This is how we find God, by letting go of everything else and by moving into the mystery, as Peter and Andrew did. It is scary, but we are made to do this. Our souls are made to walk in the dark, in pure faith. While the Eight of Cups looks empty and desolate, it speaks to an interior richness. The man leaves behind all his careful cups, but his heart is full. It is full of the mystery that whispers to us, whispers that if we leave behind everything we will be paid a hundredfold, that if we want God we must deny all other things, that we must be willing to give up much but we can trust that we will find much in return.

REFLECTIONS

- What are your first impressions of the Eight of Cups? Does this image feel peaceful? Lonely? Contemplative? Desolate?
- Have you ever felt the interior restlessness that the Eight of Cups speaks to? Did you answer the restlessness with action? If so, what did that feel like for you?
- The man in the Eight of Cups leaves behind his cups in order to heed God's call. What things in your life do you need to leave behind in order to do the same?
- In your spiritual life, have you ever felt like you were wandering around in the dark? Did it feel scary? Adventurous?
- Do you feel like God ever asked you to leave behind aspects of your life that you didn't want to give up? Did

you? Or did you find it difficult to trust that God might give you something better in return? Why?

- Reflect on the idea that we are allowed to not understand God's call, that we can follow it without fully understanding it. Does that feel comfortable for you? Or do you feel the need to understand before taking action? Why?

NINE OF CUPS

Take delight in the Lord, and he will give you the
desires of your heart. (Psalm 37:4)

Anyone who has entered deeply into the spiritual life knows that
the spiritual life can be a struggle. It's not always a struggle, though.
There are moments when we can feel God's closeness. There are
moments when, stumbling along in the darkness of faith, we are
pierced by the transcendent light of love. These moments take
many forms. Perhaps we see a beautiful work of art that makes
our spirit soar, or we read a passage of Scripture that touches us
particularly and makes us feel close to God, or the thing for which
we have long prayed is given to us in love. Something happens that
gives us joy and makes life feel less burdensome. These moments
of sweetness are spiritual consolations. They are manifestations of

grace given by God in order to draw us close to himself, and they are important in the spiritual life because they offer us a tangible feeling of God's love. The Nine of Cups offers us an image of these feelings of blessedness, the sweetness of spiritual consolation. Traditionally, the Nine of Cups is considered to be the "wish fulfillment" card of the tarot, an indication that we have received our heart's desire. A man sits in front of nine cups, representative of so many spiritual consolations. He feels as if he has been blessed, touched by God.

The man in the Nine of Cups is indeed blessed, but there is something subtly off-putting about this scene. He is almost too pleased about his blessings. The cups behind him are so proudly displayed as to nearly look like trophies. This is the understated danger of spiritual consolation. The man in the Nine of Cups has received some spiritual fulfillment, and he has fallen prey to the sneaky temptation of greed. He has started to see spiritual consolation as the goal of the spiritual life, and he is always looking for his next trophy. This man is a warning for us of the dangers of spiritual superficiality, for we are not immune to this. It is only natural that when we feel good, we want to feel good some more. We experience the sweetness of spiritual consolation, and we become possessive of this sweetness. We receive some consolation, and we are wont to start chasing the consolation instead of the Giver of the consolation. We start to want the feelings God gives us more than we want God himself. Our spiritual journeys become not journeys to God but journeys to spiritual gratification.

While the Nine of Cups is a lovely card, it asks us to hold it lightly. Spiritual consolation is a delight and balm of the spiritual life, but it is not the aim. A beautiful contemplative experience is not a prize to be won, and it is not the goal of the spiritual life. If we center our spiritual journeys around feeling good and being blessed and having all our wishes granted, we will have a tough go of things. It is a truth that God loves us very much, but it is also a truth that God is not a genie. God gives us spiritual blessings, but God does not give them according to our own wishes. We will sometimes feel the satisfaction and sweetness of the Nine of Cups, but we will likely not feel it constantly and continuously, and that is okay. God is always with us, and sometimes we feel that and sometimes we do not, and so we must learn to be grateful for consolations without clinging to them. We must joyfully take the sweetness when it comes, but we must also be on guard against centering the entirety of our spiritual lives around the sweetness. We must always love God more than we love the gifts God gives.

REFLECTIONS

- Have you ever slipped into a feeling of loving God's gifts more than you love God? Spend some time with this question; it's sometimes difficult to tease out the differences between the two.
- What are some specific examples of spiritual consolation you've experienced?
- Has spiritual consolation ever led you to pride or greed? If so, how do you think that happened?
- Spend some time with the man in this image. Does he feel relatable to you? Or off-putting? Why?
- Do you feel like the spiritual life is supposed to make you feel good all the time? If so, what might it be like to shift your perspective?
- What might it feel like to hold the Nine of Cups lightly? To take consolation when it comes without making it the aim of your spiritual life?

TEN OF CUPS

So we have known and believe the love that God has for us. God is love, and those who abide in love abide in God, and God abides in them. (1 John 4:16)

The story of Noah and his ark is one of Christianity's most well-known tales. As children, we learn about holy Noah and his holy family spared from the wrath of divine judgment. We are taught about forty days and forty nights of rain, water covering the whole earth while the animals stay warm in the ark, nestled together in sweet pairs. And we learn of the rainbow, appearing at the end of the story as the waters recede, a shining promise from God to never flood the earth again. The rainbow is a potent reminder of God's hope in us and mercy for us. It is a symbol of a covenant to love God and be loved by God, and we see this covenant played out in the Ten of Cups. So many cups form a rainbow in the sky, blessing a couple and their children and their home. God pledges faithfulness to them with cups of blessing. The Ten of Cups is an image of the ways God is lovingly attentive to us. The Beloved has seen us and we have seen the Beloved and it has changed our lives. We can expect God to care for us, to love us, to be faithful to us. Our whole lives can be lived under the protection of this blessing.

God loved us before the beginning of time, God loves us in this very moment, and God will love us for all eternity. What reaction could this knowledge provoke but exuberant praise? Truly, there is no other honest response, and this praise is what we see in the Ten of Cups. The couple, with their arms around each other, lifts their hands in praise, opening themselves to the blessings of God. Their children dance happily beside them. This is a doxological image, an expression of pure worship. It is an impulsive act, an instinct to shout about God's love from the rooftops. We fling our arms open in gratitude, without embarrassment. In the Ten of Cups, attention is given over to the God who is celebrated as the Giver of good gifts and the gracious governor of all reality. Wonder has been given, and we react with wonder, with singing and dancing and praise. This spiritual gladness is how we honor God's promise to us. It is the lively joy of a full heart, the openness of a people who know that they are loved beyond measure and feel compelled to mirror that loving attentiveness back to God.

To live under the safety and security of such blessing changes how we love God, but it also cannot help but change how we love other people. When we are this close to God, we want to be like God. We want to love the way God loves, and so we learn to love people by pouring ourselves out for them as God pours himself out for us. The two adults in the Ten of Cups, with the man embracing the woman and the woman being embraced, have extended God's love to each other. In the bearing of children, they have poured out their love into a family. In caring for their home in the world, they have poured out their love for God's creation. This is what love is. It is the nature of love that it be poured out for others. It is the nature of love that it be expressed through care. It is the nature of love that it emanates deep joy. There is joy in offering ourselves and each other and all creation to God, who has offered himself to us. The joy of the Ten of Cups is the joy of service. We cede ourselves to others, holding nothing back from the Beloved. In this way, our lives become a living sacrifice to the God who loves us beyond measure.

REFLECTIONS

- Spend some time reflecting on the story of Noah. Is it a story you give much thought to, or does it feel relegated to childhood Sunday school? What can Noah's story teach you about the love of God?
- The rainbow in the Ten of Cups stretches across the entire image, blessing everything underneath. Do you feel as if you live under God's blessing in this way? Why or why not?
- Do you feel as if offering praise to God is a normal part of your everyday life? If not, how might making time to praise God each day shift your perspective?
- What are some specific ways you can praise God today? How can you tap into the joyful praise of the Ten of Cups?
- The Ten of Cups shows us an image of God's blessing poured out through others. How can you offer a

blessing to someone today? How can you share God's love with others?

- The Ten of Cups shows us an image of two people extending God's love to other people, but also to God's creation. Do you see caring for God's creation as an act of praise? What might that look like?

ACE OF WANDS

But you will receive power when the Holy Spirit has come upon you; and you will be my witnesses in Jerusalem, in all Judea and Samaria, and to the ends of the earth. (Acts 1:8)

At the end of his earthly life, Jesus promised his followers a gift, a reminder that though his physical body would leave them, they would not be wholly abandoned. On the day of Pentecost, the disciples received this gift, the Holy Spirit descending as tongues of fire and a rushing of wind. For the disciples, this gift was a baptism into a new sort of life, a moment in which they were given both the imagination and the courage to further the Kingdom of God in new and creative ways. The Holy Spirit moved in the world then, and it moves in the world now, and it does so through us.

We see this creative vitality, this eternal moment of Pentecost, in the tarot's Ace of Wands. The Ace of Wands reminds us that the Holy Spirit was a gift to the disciples, but it is a gift for us as well. We, too, can be born again, can burst into life like so many tender budding leaves. We, too, can be made new, can grab this visionary wand, and can use it to change the world.

In the Old Testament, the book of Joel prophesies about Pentecost, telling us that "your sons and your daughters shall prophesy, your old men shall dream dreams, and your young men shall see visions" (Joel 2:28). This gift of the Holy Spirit is a gift of imagination. It is through the life-giving verdancy of the Holy Spirit that we are able to dream new and better worlds for ourselves. This cannot but fundamentally alter us; no one is unchanged by an encounter with true wonder. When we fix our eyes on the Holy Spirit, we are transformed by its glory into something more than we were before, because our imaginations are stretched beyond their finite limits. The Ace of Wands speaks to this change. This is what it feels like to encounter a creative impulse beyond ourselves, to feel the Holy Spirit as the voice inside our chests inspiring us to make art and to do good and to be alive in the world. It is the voice that tells us that it is necessary to envision a new and earnest response to the world in which we live. Our creative impulses are a most sacred thing.

The Holy Spirit gives us visions and dreams, but it also gives us the responsibility to make them reality here and now in the world in which we live. The impulse to dream is nothing without the sister impulse to create. Like Aaron's flowering staff, this wand is a budding symbol of newness and life, but it is also a symbol of the Holy Spirit as the "finger of God" in the world, pointing our creative impulses to tangible actions. The fecund vitality of the Ace of Wands is not theoretical. It begs to be made real, because the Holy Spirit does not speak on its own in the world. Our visions cannot remain mere visions. God is the Creator of all, but God made us creators, too, and it is through the Holy Spirit that we are made cocreators with God. Through the Holy Spirit we become sharers of the divine nature; we are the hands and feet of God in the world. We have a duty to bear witness to this, to bring the mystery of God into the world, to spread the kingdom of heaven here on earth. The Ace of Wands demands that we recognize and grasp the particular ways in which we are called to that mission, to see our creative impulses for the sacred gifts that they are and to place them in service to the Giver.

REFLECTIONS

- Reflect on your particular creative gifts. What are they? How can you use them for God?
- Do you feel as if you are a cocreator with God? Why or why not?
- Reflect on the story of Pentecost. How can you bring that creative energy into your own day-to-day life?
- What are some specific ways in which you can cultivate imagination and wonder in your life? How can you make more space for creativity?
- Have you ever had an experience that has made you feel reborn? If so, what was it like?
- Do you feel like you have a close relationship with the Holy Spirit? Spend some time reflecting on that relationship. What is it like?

TWO OF WANDS

Then he said to them all, "If any want to become my followers, let them deny themselves and take up their cross daily and follow me." (Luke 9:23)

In the wake of the Holy Spirit's rush of wind, the future is changed. It is a delight to have our eyes opened in this way, to be made new and to see new. The figure in the Two of Wands stands on a parapet, surveying this verdant future, this new creation. He is a young man dreaming a dream, an old man seeing a vision. This is what it feels like to be filled with the Holy Spirit, as if every possibility is suddenly and miraculously open before us. This is the moment after conversion, when we feel bright and beautiful, when we feel cleansed and full of possibility, when we feel the overwhelming impulse to follow God wherever God may take us. Here is the place where we want to follow the Holy Spirit to whatever newness the Holy Spirit would like to see. The figure in the Two of Wands is reminiscent of the Emperor in the way he firmly grasps a wand in one hand and the world in the other. It is a trace of a shadow of the Creator's power that he holds here. He has accepted the gift of cocreation, and he looks into the future as he tries to envision how things will work out.

And yet, with bliss comes longing, in a strange and subversive way. We can be filled with passion and creative energy, on fire with the love of God, enamored of the visionary power of the Holy Spirit, and we will inevitably run up against the brick wall that is the realization of what God asks of us in service to this gift. In the Two of Wands, we see a bright and beautiful future, but we also see a future that is not easy to grasp. It is a wistfulness, the place between what we would like to achieve and all we will have to give up to get there. This is a bittersweet hesitancy. Our figure is turned toward the future, but only by half. He holds the world in his hands, and yet still seems to be a bit trapped, caught by the parapet, unable to get from here to there. He looks out from his castle, world in hand, through the dream of a doorway created by these two wands, but he hasn't yet passed through. This is what it feels like to have a desire to do great things in service to God, but then to also feel a bit crestfallen at how much work it will take to achieve it. It is the space between what we are on fire to do and what we are actually willing to do.

Several of the Gospels tell a story about an encounter with Jesus and a rich young man. The young man asks Jesus how he can get to heaven. Jesus tells him to follow the commandments, and when the young man asks Jesus what else, because of course he already follows the commandments, Jesus tells him to sell all his possessions and follow him. The rich young man trudges away somewhat dejected, because to sell all one's possessions is a difficult thing, especially when one has so very many possessions. That moment is what we see in the Two of Wands. This is what happens after an encounter with the Holy Spirit, when we hold the glittering vision in one hand and the reality of sacrifice in the other. The work of the Creator demands the cooperation of the creature. The Two of Wands asks this: How much? How much of your life are you willing to change? How far can you follow that vision? What are you willing to give up in service to it? What is holding you back from following God with everything you have?

REFLECTIONS

- Reflect on the vision of the future you feel like God is calling you toward. What is it like?
- Have you ever had a conversion experience, a moment when you felt compelled to pick up your cross and follow Christ? How did you feel in the wake of it? Did it feel similar to the feelings seen in the Two of Wands?
- Has God ever called you to something which felt impossible? (Like, say, selling all your possessions?) If so, what was it? And did you heed the call?
- The suit of Wands reminds us that we get to be cocreators with God. Does that feel more like an inspiring joy or a weighty responsibility? Maybe both? Why?

- What keeps you from following God with everything you have? What holds you back? What parapet stands in your way?
- To be a cocreator with God necessarily entails chasing God's vision rather than our own. What does it feel like for you to consider giving up that kind of control?

THREE OF WANDS

Forgetting what lies behind and straining forward to what lies ahead, I press on toward the goal for the prize of the heavenly call of God in Christ Jesus. (Philippians 3:13–14)

In this earthly world, we can often feel like so many little ships in a shoreless sea, sailing around in circles with neither purpose nor destination. Life can feel as vast and overwhelming as any ocean. One of the joys of intentionally choosing God is that, in choosing God, we also choose a destination. In accepting the gift of the Holy Spirit, we also accept the gift of purpose, of a horizon toward which to steer ourselves. The Three of Wands shows us this moment. It shows us what it feels like to train our eyes on farther shores. The Holy Spirit helps us to look beyond our own limited vision, to pull back to a broader perspective so we can see the adventure of God's vision instead. The Three of Wands reminds us that this earthly world is not our home forever. Heaven is our horizon, and if we accept and commit to that, it will change the course of our lives. Is it dangerous? Perhaps. Will we always know what we're doing? Surely not. Is it full of possibility? Wonderfully so.

The figure in the Three of Wands has turned his back to us and is gazing out at the horizon. There is a sense of obedience here, of having firmly turned one's soul to God. This is the young rich man from the Gospels if he actually sold all his possessions as Jesus instructed him to do. This is Lot, who did not look back as Sodom and Gomorrah burned, but followed God in perfect trust. This is Simon Peter and Andrew dropping their fishing nets to scramble wide-eyed after Jesus. Obedience to God is its own reward. The man wears a golden circlet, as if anointed. However, with that obedience comes a sort of release as well. The man in the Three of Wands is not looking at us. He cares not at all for our approval and is wholly unconcerned with what we think. No one is there to praise him or to validate his choices. There is a particular bliss in releasing ourselves from the expectations of others, and even from our own expectations for ourselves, in order to follow instead the expectations of God.

To follow God's plan instead of our own even while living in the world—to sail the little boats of our lives toward the distant shore of heaven—can sometimes feel like too great an adventure. It requires formidable faith to live *in* the world while living *for* something altogether different, and we all have moments when we do not feel up to the task of such vulnerability. We are not left wholly abandoned to this, though. We are not alone in this journey. The man in the Three of Wands is surrounded by well-rooted wands, and he stands on a firm foundation, like that sweet parable about the house built on solid rock. We also see from the figure's outstretched arm that he is wearing armor. The Holy Spirit is a guide and an inspiration for us, but the Holy Spirit is also a protector. We are not naked in this pursuit of God's work. In the Bible, the book of Ephesians tells us about the armor of God: the breastplate of righteousness, the belt of truth, feet fitted with "whatever will make you ready to proclaim the gospel of peace" (Ephesians 6:15). We are well fitted for this work of heaven, if we choose to be. The Three of Wands offers us less worldly protection—the man stands right on the edge of his cliff—but in its stead it gives us vital joy and divine energy and the golden glow of God's love and protection.

REFLECTIONS

- In your day-to-day life, do you feel as if your eyes are trained on the horizon of heaven? Or do you easily get stuck looking at whatever's in front of you, the daily tasks and immediate problems? Why?
- Do you feel as if your faith allows you to see the world in new and exciting ways? If so, how?
- Reflect on this idea that the world is not our true home. Might that change the way you live in the world? Would it shift your perspective?
- Do you feel as if God has given you spiritual gifts to help you in this life? If so, what are they?
- Do you spend a lot of time worrying about what other people think of your choices in life? If so, how can you

train your eyes on heaven, as the man in the Three of Wands does?

- There is a strong sense of obedience in the Three of Wands, of firmly turning oneself toward the call of the Holy Spirit. Is obedience to the Holy Spirit a comfortable idea for you? Why or why not?

FOUR OF WANDS

The Lord has done great things for us, and we rejoiced.
(Psalm 126:3)

In the parable of the prodigal son, when the son finally returns home to his father after squandering his inheritance, the father is not angry. He does not scold or chastise or punish his son. When the prodigal son comes home at last, the father runs to his son, throws his arms around him, and kisses him. He dresses his son in the finest clothes, kills the fatted calf, and throws a lavish party. In this story, the father's gut reaction to his son's return is not to discipline him or turn him away or make him pay for what he has done. His deepest instinct is to offer an extravagant outpouring of love in joyful celebration of a son's homecoming. So it is with us and our Father: God loves us in the same way the father loves the prodigal son. To turn toward God—to wed ourselves to the call of the Holy Spirit's work in the world—is an act worthy of the most lavish celebration. The Four of Wands speaks to this foundational sense of celebration in the Christian life. This is what it looks like when we accept the gift of the Holy Spirit. We are deserving of this joy.

In the parable of the prodigal son, the son takes his inheritance and leaves to find freedom in the world. The paradox of the prodigal son is that he does not find it until he returns home: true freedom is found in the arms of the unconditionally loving father. We see this paradox in the Four of Wands as well. Two people emerge from a walled town in the distance into an open space framed by a flowering canopy. In this open space, there is more vulnerability, because accepting the Holy Spirit's call necessarily requires letting go of the things that offer us protection in this world, things like wealth and power. But in moving away from worldly protection, these people have also moved away from worldly expectations. There is more life here in the open, and more abundance. This is what it feels like to be set free by the Holy Spirit, to "walk at liberty, for I have sought your precepts" (Psalm 119:45). When we root our lives in the joy of the Holy Spirit, life feels less like a cutthroat competition for worldly prestige and more like an extravagant feast. What we accept in welcoming the vocation of Christian life is unconditional love, and with that love comes unburdened freedom.

Behind the couple in the Four of Wands are yet more people following them into loving freedom. This sense of true celebration is irresistible. We all want to feel this kind of love. We all want to feel this kind of freedom. We all want to be embraced and welcomed home. The Four of Wands asks us if our work in the world as Christians captures that sense of belonging. It presses us to remember that joy is also a fruit of the Spirit and should not be an afterthought in the lives we live. It reminds us that to further the Kingdom of God in the world is work, to be sure, but to further the Kingdom of God in the world should also be a good time, or else what's the point? The Gospel is good news, after all. We get to live under the flowering protection of the Father's eternal and unconditional love. The Lord has done great things for us, and we are called to live in celebration of that fact. Everything we do can and should point to the joy of the prodigal son's return, the joy of God's exquisite love for us.

REFLECTIONS

- Reflect on the story of the prodigal son. Have you ever felt the kind of joyful love the son receives from the father? Have you ever given that kind of love? How does giving and receiving that kind of love change you?
- What does your faith community do to celebrate people who come into the faith? What can you do to extend that sense of celebration?
- The Four of Wands speaks to the ways in which joy is contagious, drawing people to it. How can you, as a Christian, foster that sense of contagious joy within your faith?
- Reflect on the ways in which you feel called to further the Kingdom of God in the world. Do they feel rooted in joy and celebration? Why or why not?
- The Four of Wands speaks to the freedom of accepting the call of the Holy Spirit. Do you feel a

sense of freedom in the Christian life? Why or why not?

- Do you feel as if God has done great things for you? Things worthy of praise? Things that make you feel like a beloved prodigal child? If so, what are they?

FIVE OF WANDS

And let us consider how to provoke one another to
love and good deeds, not neglecting to meet together,
as is the habit of some, but encouraging one another,
and all the more as you see the Day approaching.
(Hebrews 10:24–25)

Sainthood never comes easily. To grow in virtue is not always
natural for us, and yet we are called to this growth all the same.
When we accept the gift of the Holy Spirit, we accept the grow-
ing pains as well. Sainthood is a thing that must be practiced, and
ideally, the Christian community is a safe and forgiving place in
which to do this. The Five of Wands shows us what this looks
like, Christian life as a place of productive training, a working
out of one's sainthood. It is in Christian community that we are

able to make mistakes and ask questions and grow in God's love. This is where we work through those growing pains of grace, though the work is a delicate balance. None of us are perfect, so while God is present, where two or three are gathered in his name, conflict is sure to be present as well. This conflict does not have to be negative, though. It gives us an opportunity to practice courtesy and respect, to extend love toward each other, to exercise the gifts of the Holy Spirit. We must practice sainthood to grow in sainthood, and so we spar together, and in doing so, we polish ourselves in virtue.

Our zeal to follow God is a healthy impulse, but like all healthy impulses, it can fall into intemperance. A desire for virtue can easily turn into obsessive rule-following and finger-pointing. We want to nitpick other people for not following all the right rules, for not looking for God in the right places, for not praying or giving or seeking in the right way. Sometimes this petty fighting can feel like the work of the Spirit, but it is not. It is a kind of false Pentecost, thrilling to the person doing the scolding but certainly not producing any actual creative work of the Spirit. In the Waite-Smith Five of Wands, it is difficult to tell whether these figures are playing or fighting, and that is the point. It is so easy for a well-intentioned desire for virtue to tip into vainglory. It is so easy to use our God-given intelligences and skills to further our own selves rather than God. It is so easy for our actions to become directed toward glory instead of love. The suit of Wands is full of the creative work of the Holy Spirit, but when we lose that sense of the Spirit, we descend into mere ego-driven fighting. The healthy tussling of the Five of Wands becomes tense unrest.

There is a story in the Gospels about Jesus walking in on the disciples having an argument. He asks them what they're fighting about, and they abashedly admit that they were arguing about who was the greatest. There is a strange comfort in this, in knowing that Jesus's disciples were also prone to this competition of virtue. Even the apostles bickered about who was the best among them. Even the disciples had trouble distinguishing righteous tussling from petty infighting. These men and women were devoted to God, but the competition was still there, sowing division. It is easy to confuse piosity with piety; this is the deliberate ambiguity of the Five of Wands. In the story, Jesus does not scold the disciples for arguing over who is the best. Jesus does remind them that he came to serve, and that they are called to follow this example of service. Our desire for sainthood—our desire to further the Kingdom of God—should always flow from a place of love, not judgment. We must turn to each other in love, not competition. We are not called to cut each other down, but to help each other grow.

REFLECTIONS

- Do you feel that it is important for a Christian community to be a safe place for questions? If so, how do you think Christianity can do that?
- How do you practice sainthood in your own life? How do you lead others to sainthood?
- Reflect on your feelings about conflict. Do you see conflict as an opportunity for growth and connection? Or as an opportunity to prove your rightness? Why?
- How can you work to create a Christian community of love and connection in your own life? How can you extend that grace to others?
- Have you ever felt your own desire for virtue slide into a desire for praise and rightness? If so, how can

you correct those moments? How can you return to connection?

- The Five of Wands reminds us that we are not called to be right, but to be compassionate. How can you foster that sense of servanthood in your daily life?

SIX OF WANDS

In him you also, when you had heard the word of
truth, the gospel of your salvation, and had believed in
him, were marked with the seal of the promised Holy
Spirit; this is the pledge of our inheritance toward
redemption as God's own people, to the praise of his
glory. (Ephesians 1:13–14)

Pentecost was, in many ways, an unveiling. In a particular blazing
moment in time, tongues of fire descended and the disciples' eyes
were opened to the possibility of all they could be. Baptized with
fire, they were given the gift of sharing in some small part in the
glory of God. While Pentecost was a specific moment in time, it
exists outside of time as well, and it is an act in which we all have a

share. We can be transformed in this way, too, if we choose to be. Jesus's disciples were made new, and so are we. The apostles prophesied a new world, and so can we. The glory of the Holy Spirit is our glory, too. If we accept the gift of the Holy Spirit, our eyes will be opened to our own inherent dignity as children of God, and the Six of Wands gives us an interpretation of this feeling. When we take up the practice of virtue to which the Holy Spirit has called us, we see our own sacredness and we carry ourselves differently. Tongues of fire light the darkness and show us how God sees us. This is the way we should be in the world: confident, rooted in the knowledge of the inherent holiness of the human person, never forgetting who we are.

At first glance, the Six of Wands seems to be a traditional image of victory, a champion riding his steed through an adoring crowd. The Six of Wands is indeed about success and triumph and exaltation, but it is also, somewhat paradoxically, a reminder of the ways in which our victories should not center us. There is a temptation sometimes to feel like our victories are singular things, belonging only to us and executed in a vacuum. But that is far from the truth, particularly in the Christian life. There are two laurel wreaths in this image: one on the victor's head, and one on his wand. His triumph belongs to him, but it also belongs to God. When we are gifted with the Holy Spirit, we enter into active cooperation with God. We become cocreators with God in the world. Our victories are never solely our own; our triumphs are always shared with the God who gives us the ability to triumph. The glory of the Six of Wands is virtue. Virtue by definition exalts God above oneself, and so the victory of the Six of Wands is not a thing we can or should claim solely for ourselves.

The Six of Wands calls us to recognize our own dignity in

God, but also to recognize the dignity of God in others. We share this gift of the Holy Spirit, and so the sense of victory we feel here is a sense of belonging as well. Our victor in this image is not alone; he rides his steed through a crowd of people celebrating him. However, the people in this crowd are not without their own wands. They are not without their own gifts. We are all victors. None of us are without glory. None of us are without dignity, and the triumph of the Christian life is in our recognition of this. It is in community that we see the glory of the Holy Spirit in its fullness—in lifting up others and being lifted up ourselves. Our victories belong to God, but our victories also belong to each other. We all have our gifts, and we are called to share in each other's victories, to lift each other up in turn. In our time and energy, our tears and laughter, hour after hour and day after day, we are made to show each other the comfort of belonging, the sharing of our inheritance of God's love.

REFLECTIONS

- Who do you relate to more in this image? The man on the horse or one of the people in the crowd? Why?
- Do you feel as if you share in the glory of the Holy Spirit? Why or why not?
- In what ways can you thank God for the successes in your life? How can you cultivate that gratitude?
- Reflect on the idea of Christian community as a place to lift each other up. Has that been your experience of Christian community? Why or why not?

- How can you pour yourself out for someone today? How can you lift someone up? How can you make someone feel like the man on the horse in the Six of Wands?
- How can you lift up yourself today? How can you cultivate a sense of your own claim on the glory of the Holy Spirit?

SEVEN OF WANDS

... so that the genuineness of your faith—being more precious than gold that, though perishable, is tested by fire—may be found to result in praise and glory and honor when Jesus Christ is revealed. (1 Peter 1:7)

It is easy to enjoy the Christian life as long as it does not ask too much of us, as long as it remains comfortable and safe. It is easy to say our prayers and go to church on Sundays and give here and there, but few of us are willing to upend our entire lives for God. Sometimes God insists, though. If we accept the call to be cocreators with God in this world—if we accept the gift of the Holy Spirit—we have to accept all of it, and it is God's prerogative to give us tasks that seem beyond our power to handle. God often asks much more of us than we feel comfortable giving, and we see the discomfort of this in the Seven of Wands. The man in this image has his one wand, and that is nice. He is enjoying that gift, but he does not want any more. Perhaps he feels unqualified for this work. Perhaps he does not want to change his life quite so much. Perhaps he just wants comfort and safety, but God never promises us ease, and God often believes in us much more than we believe in ourselves. The wand this man holds is his, but the wands pointed at him are also his, and if he accepts the one, he must accept them all.

God believes that we can do great things, but we struggle mightily against this trust, and the Bible gives us many stories of people attempting to refuse God's plans. Moses tells God that he is not eloquent enough to lead the Israelites out of Egypt. Jonah tries to run away from his call to prophesy in Nineveh and is famously swallowed by a whale over his fleeing. Jesus himself, in the garden of Gethsemane, does not deny the Father but does pray with blood and sweat and tears for the Father to "remove this cup from me" (Luke 22:42). This internal struggle we see in the Seven of Wands is deeply relatable. The man in this image is not enjoying this process of accepting God's enormous grace. This fierce balking is understandable, but the best use of our energy is perhaps not in willing that God ask less of us than he does, but in accepting that the work of following God in the world is not all comfort and joy. The Holy Spirit is a peaceful dove, but the Holy Spirit is also a refining fire. Holiness can feel like a dreadful thing, and there will almost always be a certain amount of fear and trembling and gnashing of teeth in the process of becoming the people whom God believes we can be.

The figure in the Seven of Wands is backed up against a cliff. It may be, in fact, the same cliff we see the Fool joyfully leaping from at the very start of the tarot. The Fool easily abandons all to follow God; he is a beautiful example in that way. The man in the Seven of Wands gives us a more honest look at what following God's will often feels like. Sometimes we are able to leap easily. Sometimes we must be pushed by so many wands. But if we say yes to God, we must say yes to all that God may ask of us, and it is the only way off the cliff, no matter how it happens. It is in letting go of our own assumptions about our abilities that we hold on to God's plan. It is in detaching ourselves from our own wills that we accept God's will. We can hold the one wand on our own. We cannot hold the other six without the help of God. "Obedience" is an unpopular word these days, but in the end, we must be obedient to the call, no matter how insurmountable it may seem.

REFLECTIONS

- Do you feel as if God has ever called you to something you don't feel smart enough or powerful enough or capable enough to do? How did you react?
- Reflect on the idea of the Holy Spirit as a refining fire. In your own life, do you feel the Holy Spirit more as a peacemaker or a fiery refiner? How does your perception of the Holy Spirit change your relationship to it?
- Do you feel as if it is always easy to follow God's will? Or do you feel like you sometimes have to be pushed there like the man in the Seven of Wands? Why?
- Can you recall a time when the Holy Spirit pushed you out of your comfort zone? What was that like for you? Did you go obediently or did you feel more like the man in the Seven of Wands?

- Reflect on the idea of obedience. How does the idea of obedience make you feel? Why?
- Do you feel as if you pick and choose the aspects of Christian life that feel most comfortable to you, holding on to the parts that are easy for you and ignoring the rest? If so, how can you more fully abandon yourself to God's call?

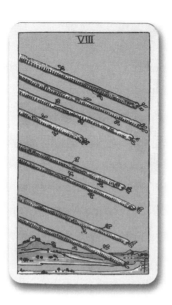

EIGHT OF WANDS

God added his testimony by signs and wonders and various miracles, and by gifts of the Holy Spirit, distributed according to his will. (Hebrews 2:4)

Moses heard God's voice in a burning bush that was not consumed. The Israelites were fed in the desert by manna raining down from heaven. God was made man, born of a virgin. Jesus walked on water and multiplied loaves and fishes and raised people from the dead. To be a Christian is to believe in miracles, to recognize that God moves through the immovable world, to know that the Holy Spirit gives us "signs and wonders" (Acts 14:3). Miracles are gifts brought into the world—gifts for us—but they are acquired in a way that is wholly beyond our understanding. The natural rules do not apply, and we certainly do not understand the unnatural rules.

This seems obvious—of course we do not understand God!—but it is easy for us to convince ourselves otherwise. It is easy to accept only what we understand, hide everything else away in some dusty corner, and call that Christianity. Hubris creeps in unnoticed, and the Eight of Wands shuts it down abruptly. It is a strange image: there are, noticeably, no people here. These wands are rushing in on the world, quick and mysterious and unrestrainable. God will break into the world, and we cannot stop this and we cannot understand this, but we can accept the gift if we are humble and brave.

We are called to let mystery pierce us, change us and change the world, but must we accept this terrifying gift? It would have been easier for Moses to run away from the burning bush. It would have been easier for Mary to say no to Gabriel. It is easier, in some ways, to not believe in miracles, to brush them off as nonsense. We might like to ignore God's vision and God's mystery and God's terrible power, but we are braver than all that. Mystery knocks at the door. Vision sniffs at the edges of the heart, whining to be let in. These things cannot comfortably be ignored, not really. Moses spoke to the burning bush. The Israelites ate the manna. Mary said yes to the angel Gabriel's request. Miracles happened and were accepted as miracles. While we do not see ourselves in the Eight of Wands—the whole landscape is taken up by God's terrible grace hurtling through the air, miracle crashing into the dull, cruel sameness of the world—the wands are still for us. The mystery is for us. A miracle breaks through, longing to be caught, and to catch it is part of our work in the world.

God works through us in this world, but it is God's work we are doing and not ours, and God's work is often mysterious to us. We do not like the unknown, generally speaking. It is frightening to open ourselves to a vision we cannot fully grasp with the intellect. Miracles are uncomfortable because they remind us that we will never understand God. Understanding God is not the point, though. We cannot in good faith call ourselves Christians and also carefully shut out the Holy Spirit's mysterious fire. It might make us feel safer, but God does not play it safe. To do God's good work in the world, we must be brave enough to approach the mystery. If we are to accept this terrible, hurtling gift, we must let our whole selves be placed with absolute faith in a mystery we will never understand. We must let go of our insistence on absolute control and understanding. We must get out of our own way, no matter how wildly disorienting it may feel. We must be always ready to take off our sandals and stand on holy ground, to say yes to an angel's call, to humble ourselves before all God can do, to accept miracles. It is terrifying, but it is an adventure too, to hold our hands open for these mysterious wands in pure reception.

REFLECTIONS

- Do you believe in miracles? Do you think that Christians are required to believe in miracles? Why or why not?
- Have you ever experienced something miraculous? If so, do you feel like it changed the nature of your faith? In what ways?
- Reflect on the idea that the Holy Spirit moves and breathes in the world. What does that feel like for you? Strange? Comforting?
- Hebrews 2:4 tells us that the gifts of the Holy Spirit are distributed according to God's will, not our own. Do you feel like you've ever been given a gift you didn't

necessarily want? Have you had to catch a wand that didn't necessarily feel like yours? If so, what was it like?

- What would it feel like for you to move through life expecting miracles, looking for them always?
- How can you cultivate an openness to miracles in your own life? How can you be brave enough to accept as real the presence of the Holy Spirit's power in the world?

NINE OF WANDS

Be alert at all times, praying that you may have the
strength to escape all these things that will take place,
and to stand before the Son of Man. (Luke 21:36)

In the Gospel of Luke, Jesus tells a parable about a master and his
servants. The master is at a wedding banquet, and the servants wait
with bated breath for him to return. They are dressed for action
and they have their lamps lit so as to be ready to throw open the
door for their master as soon as he comes home. The point of this
parable lies in the watchfulness. The disciples were told, "Blessed
are those slaves whom the master finds alert when he comes"
(Luke 12:37). Jesus urged his followers to faith and to action, but
he also urged them to stay awake. He told his disciples that he
would return again, but at "an unexpected hour" (Luke 12:40),

and so vigilance was a necessary virtue. It is necessary for us still. Part of our Christian work in the world is keeping ourselves spiritually alert, and the Nine of Wands gives us an image of this. We cannot resign ourselves to the world, because our work is the work of God in the world; the work of God in the world is love, and love and resignation cannot coexist. We must be like servants always ready—with lamps lighted and sandals tied—for their master to return from the wedding.

This kind of vigilance was not easy for Jesus's disciples then, and it is not easy for us now. We see this struggle in the Nine of Wands, in the figure's bandaged head and set expression, in the way he has obviously put up a mighty fight to remain alert where he stands. We must stay awake in order to guard our hearts and keep the faith, but the temptation to fall asleep always lies in wait. In some ways, remaining alert feels more difficult now than it ever has before. We live in a world filled with so many distractions, so many easy diversions. The overwhelming and frenetic busyness of modern life can easily breed a sort of spiritual stupor, a dullness of soul that must be fought back. The sheer volume of information we absorb every day creates a kind of static in our souls, through which it is difficult to hear the master's coming. We become distracted, we forget to keep watch, and we fall asleep. Jesus knew this difficulty, and he warned against it, telling his disciples, "Be on guard so that your hearts are not weighed down with dissipation and drunkenness and the worries of this life" (Luke 21:34). It is a fight to stay awake, but our faith must be something worth staying awake for, or it is no faith at all.

Jesus knew this task of remaining vigilant would be difficult for us, and he did not leave us alone to it. In his infinite compassion, he sent the Holy Spirit to the disciples. The task of the Holy Spirit was to help the disciples grow in faith and to help them to grow others in faith, but also to help them remain awake and watchful, to protect them from this spiritual sleepiness that so easily overtakes us even today. Indeed, part of the work of the Holy Spirit in the world is to predispose us to welcome Christ in faith, to keep us awake so that we are always ready to open the door for him. We see the Holy Spirit's protection in the Nine of Wands. The figure uses one wand to fight back attacks, but he has used the others to create a sort of rampart. These wands are planted securely behind him, protecting him like so many little soldiers on guard. When Jesus proclaimed the coming of the Holy Spirit, he called it the Paraclete, literally "helper." The Holy Spirit is our protector and advocate in this life. We must protect ourselves from this desire to sleep, to let the easy way of the world overtake us, but we have the Holy Spirit at our side. If we hold fast to the Spirit, we cannot fall asleep. If we accept the gift of the Holy Spirit, we accept a presence to protect us.

REFLECTIONS

- Reflect on the idea that we are called to watchfulness in this life. What does spiritual watchfulness look like to you?
- Do you find it easy to remain watchful like the servants in the parable? Or are you prone to fall asleep? Why?
- What things in your life tend to distract you from God's presence, causing you to lose vigilance? How can you change them?
- Do you ever ask God to help you stay alert to his presence? Is that something you feel comfortable doing? Why or why not?

- Reflect on the idea of the Holy Spirit as Paraclete. Do you see the Holy Spirit as a protector? Why or why not?

- 1 Peter 5:8 is another verse that cautions us to remain vigilant, reminding us that the Devil prowls around like a roaring lion. Is protecting yourself from the Devil a part of your spiritual life? How can the Holy Spirit help you to protect yourself so you can do God's work in the world?

TEN OF WANDS

For we have become partners of Christ, if only we
hold our first confidence firm to the end.
(Hebrews 3:14)

The story of Pentecost is a dramatic one, all fire and wind, miracle
and light. Jesus's disciples were kissed by the Holy Spirit, reas-
sured that God was still with them, and given gifts to continue
Jesus's work in the world. This was a singular moment of glory,
but after the Holy Spirit comes upon us, we are left with the
commitment. After the wedding comes the marriage. After we
are given the gift, we must serve it, and the service can sometimes
feel like a burden. It can sometimes feel like a bore. The Ten of
Wands speaks to this burden and bore. Our figure holds a bundle
of wands in his arms; there are so many that he is bent over from

the weight of them as he trudges along. He does trudge along, though. He does not stop. He does not drop the wands. He does not grumble. He recognizes that the work of God in the world is love, that love—real love—is a commitment, and that commitment isn't always fantastical. The work of God in the world cannot be an endless series of dramatic mountaintop moments or miraculous acts. Like any marriage, it is mostly made of small moments of love, of commitment to goodness even when it is unseen, of being in it for the long haul. The weight of glory does not always feel like glory, but that does not make it unimportant.

As the Ten of Wands is the last card in the suit of Wands, it would make sense for it to represent some sort of ending or completion. It does not give us that satisfaction, though, and it can feel like an annoyance. We want to see the end result of our hard labor, but the work of God in the world is a living thing. It is not subject to our attempts at goal setting. We want success, but God continually gives us new problems to solve, new occasions for thought and for action and for service and for love. The timeline of the Kingdom of God does not belong to us. We are cocreators with God, and any artist knows that the work of being an artist never ends. The work is unending and perpetual, and we all have a share in it. This is what the Ten of Wands attempts to impress upon us. We are never finished with being God's hands and feet in the world. Eternal love means eternal commitment. We must simply do the work and know that we do not control its completion.

For all the weight of glory and burden of responsibility, this is not an unhappy image. The sky is bright blue. The man is slowly making his way home, and home seems not far off. The path is clear, and he will reach his destination, though he cannot see it for all the wands he carries. The Ten of Wands reminds us that we must do the work, but it also reminds us of what we are working toward, which is the Kingdom of God. And so of course there is work and of course there is burden and of course it is a yoke. But it takes us home. The work of God in the world demands a heroic effort, but it is an effort for something truly meaningful, and that makes all the difference. There is a joyfulness in being allowed to be a servant of the work, to know that what we are doing is purposeful. It is not all dramatic Pentecost moments, but the work means something all the same, and that makes the burden light.

REFLECTIONS

- Do you recognize yourself in this image? What feelings does it bring up for you?
- Reflect on the idea of commitment to God as being similar to a marriage, which is built on the small things. Can you see your work as cocreator with God in this way? Not always fantastical but instead made up of consistent, daily effort? Can you still find meaning in that? Why or why not?
- The Ten of Wands is not an unhappy image, even though it does speak to burden. Can you see your own life in this way? Can you find the joy in the burden? Do you think that would make your burdens feel lighter? Why or why not?
- Reflect on the idea that our commitment to God's work does not end in this life. How does that make you feel?
- What are some ways in which you can draw strength for carrying the weight of glory in this world? How can you hold your confidence firm to the end?

- The Ten of Wands remind us, at the end of the fiery and passionate suit of Wands, that we are not the protagonists of God's story. We are here to further God's glory, not our own. What does that idea feel like for you?

6

THE COURT CARDS

Each of the four suits of the minor arcana has four court cards: the Page, the Knight, the Queen, and the King. While they are part of the minor arcana, they have their own section in this book because they don't quite lead into or follow on from the numbered cards of each suit. Instead, they show us each suit's energy within the hands of different people, the varying ways in which the theme of each suit can manifest in a person's life. The sixteen court cards of the tarot represent a wide variety of personalities. They are, by turns, meek and quiet, assertive and energetic, interior and contemplative, bold and striking. They are leaders and thinkers, contemplatives and go-getters. And in this book each of these court cards represents a holy person of God, a man or woman who lived a life of exemplary faith from which we can draw spiritual inspiration. The court cards are a re- minder of the myriad ways in which we can live the Christian truth in the world. It is easy sometimes to fall into an idea that there is, some- how, an "ideal" Christian. The truth, though, is that the kingdom of heaven takes all kinds, from the sweet and affectionate Page of Cups to the bold and fiery King of Wands and everything in between. The court cards show us the tiniest sliver of the communion of Christian life, and they remind us that there are many ways to be holy.

PAGE OF PENTACLES

Pure holy simplicity confounds all the wisdom of this
world and the wisdom of the flesh. (Francis of Assisi)

Francis of Assisi, one of Christianity's most beloved saints, was a friar who lived in twelfth-century Italy. He grew up in a comfortable and wealthy home, but as a young man renounced his family's wealth and embraced a simple life lived in service to God, eventually founding the Franciscan order. He lived humbly, preaching to whomever would listen (even if it was just the birds) of the virtue of poverty and finding joy in the simplicity of daily life and the gift of God's creation.

The tarot's Page of Pentacles owns little. He has no horse like the Knight does, and he has no throne like the Queen does, and he has no castle like the King does. He stands in the open air, unencumbered by the weight of wealth or power, tilting up a graceful foot as if he might at any moment leap outside the bounds of the image. All he holds is a coin, and he holds it so lightly that it looks like it might fall from his fingertips. This Page is poor, but he is also free. He has found liberty in his chosen poverty, just as Francis did. After growing up in a wealthy family, Francis deliberately chose to remove himself from that wealth, and he lived into the simplicity of his life in dramatic ways. He called himself Il Poverello ("the little poor one"), and he made poverty a hallmark of the Franciscan order. This is how we know Francis best: a man wearing the coarse brown robe of a friar, sleeping under the stars, relying on the kindness of strangers—poor, but free.

Poor, but free, and also happy. It's easy to imagine a man living in poverty as a dour ascetic, but while Francis was deadly serious about his calling, he was anything but sullen. He is, in fact, particularly known for being a saint of infectious joy. He did not grumble about his poverty, and he chided fellow friars who walked around with downcast faces. He knew how to be persistently joyful even in dustiness and hunger, teaching us a lesson about the joy that comes not from possessions but from God. There is a difference between the fleeting happiness of material goods and the deep and abiding joy of living in faith, and while we see this played out in the life of Francis, we see it in the Page of Pentacles as well. The Page of Pentacles has so little to his name, and he is smiling. For us, who live in a culture that constantly tells us that more stuff will make us happy, this seems shocking. It is a necessary shock, though, to be reminded of how little we truly need and where true joy comes from.

Unencumbered by the complications of stuff and filled to the brim with childlike joy as a result, the Page of Pentacles is able to see magic in the kinds of things that often slip our notice. He stands directly in the middle of the bounty of God's creation.

The simplicity of chosen poverty allows him to see that the trees are a miracle, the mountains are a miracle, and every tender shoot coming up from the lovingly tended garden is a miracle. The Page of Pentacles and Francis are kindred spirits in this way. Francis's love of nature is perhaps the most well-known and celebrated fact of his life. He wasn't a pantheist; he wouldn't have even called himself a mystic. He preached that the way to God is always through the church and the sacraments, but he also preached that God's gifts are present everywhere. Francis saw the glory of God in the birds and the butterflies and the bees, in Brother Sun and Sister Moon. It's a heart-opening way of interacting with the world, and it seems that Saint Francis and the Page of Pentacles would tell us the same thing: live simply, hold on to joy, and look for God wherever you are.

REFLECTIONS

- Understanding that we can't all be Franciscans, how can you cultivate the virtue of poverty in your own life?
- Reflect on the lightness and freedom of the Page of Pentacles. Does that kind of freedom feel relatable or accessible to you? Or do you feel burdened by your life? Why?
- Where in nature do you feel most connected to God? Where do you find God in the natural world? Is the natural world an important part of your spirituality, as it was for Francis?
- Though Francis was an expert, he maintained a simple and childlike pleasure that can be difficult to tap into as

an adult. What are some specific ways in which you can hold on to childlike joy in your life?

- Francis, like a child, fully relied on God for his well-being. Do you feel like you do the same? Why or why not? Where do you hold on to control?
- Spend some time thinking about what Francis called "holy simplicity." What does that mean to you? Do you think of holiness as a complicated thing?

KNIGHT OF PENTACLES

Saint Joseph did not do extraordinary things, but rather by the constant practice of ordinary and common virtues, he attained that sanctity which elevates him above all the other saints.
(Joseph Marello)

Saint Joseph, husband to Mary and earthly father to Jesus, is a man we all know. He is also a man to whom it is easy to pay no mind. A steady presence in the Gospels, he is a somewhat hidden presence, too. We know only the barest facts about him: he took care of Mary, he was a paternal figure for Jesus, and he was a carpenter in the little village of Nazareth. His vocation lay not in extraordinary feats of daring but in a hidden and responsible faithfulness, in moving quietly in the background of the drama played out around him, in taking care of those who had a grander part to play. The sainthood of Joseph is the sainthood of dependability. It is the sainthood of the supporting role. It is the sainthood of the ordinary.

The Knight of Pentacles is unusual among the Knights of the tarot. While the other Knights ride warhorses built for combat, the Knight of Pentacles rides a draft horse built for slow and steady work. He stands not on the battlefield but among his farm fields, carefully plowed and ready for planting. Someone has to be on the frontline—and plenty of people are well suited for that—but the Knight of Pentacles is far more interested in the slow and steady work of caretaking. What saint better represents this idea than Joseph? Joseph is one of the greatest of saints, and his greatness lies in his ability to take responsibility for the people who were placed in his care. Joseph's vocation was marriage and fatherhood, loving his wife and loving his son. And like the Knight of Pentacles' careful cultivation of his fields, Joseph took it seriously.

Farming is not the kind of work that happens all at once in a blaze of furious glory. It is, rather, the kind of work that requires daily labor. The life of the Knight of Pentacles is nothing more and nothing less than the accumulation of a million small and hidden labors: plowing fields, planting seeds, harvesting crops, doing it all again in the next season and in the season after that. His life is not a life of fame and excitement, but a life of quiet tending. It is a life of showing up for the small jobs and finding sanctity in the smallness. Joseph, too, reminds us that there is little glory in caretaking. It is rarely a grand and dramatic thing. Perhaps this is why we know so little about him. Perhaps his life seems so ordinary as to be barely worth mentioning. And yet, he is still a saint. He reminds us that there is holiness in the acts of care so ordinary that they are barely worth mentioning. Joseph showed up for the small labors, and we can, too.

In both the Knight of Pentacles and in the life of Saint Joseph, we see a cultivation of dependable nurturing. A life of quiet care, however, is not a life that lacks fortitude. The Knight of Pentacles, like all the Knights of the tarot, is courageous. It is simply a different kind of courage we see here. Though it is quieter and less dramatic, it is no less important for that. Joseph had the courage to protect Mary's reputation as an unwed mother. He had the courage to raise Jesus as his own son. He had the courage to enter into a story he did not fully understand and to show up each day to provide for those in his care. Joseph, and the Knight of Pentacles, remind us that there is courage in the small things too, in the deep and abiding faithfulness of a quiet life.

REFLECTIONS

- Do you ever feel as if your life is not exciting enough? Do you ever feel like your life is too ordinary to be truly holy? What might it feel like to lean into the ordinariness and try to find holiness there?
- Who are the people in your care? How can you bring Joseph's quiet and patient spirit to your caretaking?
- The Knight of Pentacles finds sanctity in the smallest labors of each day. How can you do the same? Do you think you can find holiness in laundry and dirty dishes and quiet moments of caretaking that no one else sees?
- Joseph became a great saint not through extraordinary acts but through the accumulation of small virtues. Does this idea make holiness feel more accessible for you? Why or why not?

- Who has been a Knight of Pentacles for you in your life? Who has offered you quiet and dependable caretaking? How did that caretaking feel for you?
- Reflect on your ideas about courage. Do you see courage in the Knight of Pentacles? In the life of Joseph? Why or why not?

QUEEN OF PENTACLES

The Word is living, being, spirit, all verdant greening, all creativity. This Word manifests itself in every creature. (Hildegard of Bingen)

It's difficult to point to the thing Hildegard of Bingen is most well-known for, because Hildegard was so many things: abbess, philosopher, composer, mystic, visionary, herbalist. A polymath of the High Middle Ages, she invented her own constructed language, wrote what is arguably the earliest example of a morality play, and is considered by many to be the founder of scientific natural history in Germany. From a young age, she had mystical visions of God's creation, but she also had a practical curiosity about the natural world. It is the marriage of these two views that connects Hildegard so well to the Queen of Pentacles and what makes her so special among the saints.

Seated in front of a lush and verdant landscape and surrounded by a bough of roses, the Queen of Pentacles lives deeply in touch with the natural world. Creation is her home, a gift to enjoy. This comfortable connection is also present in Hildegard's theology, which is centered around the harmony of the created world and its relation to God. In Hildegard's view, nature was God's greatest achievement. She believed that God gave us the ability to enjoy the natural world for a reason. God delights in what he creates, and we can delight in it, too. Hildegard did just that. In her writing, she compares the Eucharist to a chick springing from an egg, or a butterfly emerging from a chrysalis. She represents God's love as the sun's rays piercing the shadows. Evocative images of the natural world abound in Hildegard's writing: perfume and greenness, jacinth and diamonds, swift stag and pure water. Like the Queen of Pentacles, Hildegard viewed all things through the lens of God's abundant creation.

This concept of abundance, so clearly seen in the Queen of Pentacles, is also present in Hildegard's many works, both mystical and scientific. We see this perhaps most clearly in the concept of *viriditas*. *Viriditas* is a Latin word, roughly translated as "greenness," "fecundity," or "youthful freshness." The word itself is not Hildegard's invention, but it is associated with her because she used it so frequently in her works. Hildegard believed that, as God nourishes the earth, so God also nourishes our lives. *Viriditas* is what this nourishment looked like to Hildegard, a nourishment created and preserved by God. For Hildegard, *viriditas* was a growth of spirituality that was achieved only by the presence of God in one's life, and it went beyond mere ideas about freshness and verdure. In Hildegard's theological worldview, it represented the complex relationship between the created and the Creator, to be the created nourished by the Creator. To be loved by God is to live as the Queen of Pentacles, nestled among fresh greenness all our days.

The Queen of Pentacles lives in a world of *viriditas,* but she's also a deeply grounded and nurturing figure among the court cards. Hers is an abundance that you can reach out and touch, and Hildegard lived in that same space. Hildegard had a highly mystical view of God's creation, but she also had more pragmatic leanings. For Hildegard, a practical study of the natural world would have been just as much an act of praise as the telling of her mystical visions. She had a great determination to communicate the workings of the earth, and she compiled two substantial scientific works to that end. The *Physica* is a set of nine books listing almost a thousand plants and animals in German, describing their physical and medicinal properties, and *Causae et Curae* examines the causes and cures of diseases, relating them to a sort of allegorical physiology and offering remedies. For both Hildegard and the Queen of Pentacles, God's creation was as functional as it was mystical, an awe-inspiring gift, but also a thing to understand and to use and to enjoy to its most lush fullness.

REFLECTIONS

- Is your view of the natural world more mystical or practical? Why?
- Do you feel as if being present in nature is an act of praise to God, as Hildegard did? Why or why not?
- Hildegard believed that the "Word manifests itself in every creature." Spend some time with this idea. Do you believe it to be true? Why or why not?

- Do you consider yourself to be a part of the natural world or separate from it? How does it feel to think of yourself as one of the many beloved creatures of the Creator?
- Reflect on the idea that the natural world is a gift for us, given by God. Does that change the intention with which you act toward the natural world? Why or why not?
- Where can you cultivate the concept of *viriditas* in your own life?

KING OF PENTACLES

He should first show them in deeds rather than words
all that is good and holy. (Benedict of Nursia)

Benedict of Nursia was born in fifth-century Italy, his life
tumbling into the disintegration of the Roman Empire. The son
of a Roman noble, he spent his youth studying in Rome but hated
the immorality he saw there and fled as soon as he could. He spent
several years as a hermit, and the simple solitude of that time had a
profound impact on both his faith and the course of his life. Benedict went on to found thirteen monasteries, including the great
Benedictine monastery of Monte Cassino. The Father of Western
Monasticism, Benedict is most well-known for his *Rule of Saint
Benedict,* a set of regulations he wrote for the monks under his

care. Benedict lived a life of great care, both deliberate and God-focused, and his *Rule,* echoing through generations, generously teaches us to do the same.

The King of Pentacles lives by the rule of simplicity. His earthly possessions are few, and he sits outside the walls of his palace, pulled more toward the simple rhythms of nature than whatever is happening in the castle behind him. The King of Pentacles finds God in the tending to and enjoyment of his grapevines, in the self-discipline of work and rest, in cultivating the gift and giving thanks for it. We see this same spirit in Saint Benedict, who lived by the pastoral practice of *ora et labora,* "pray and work." Benedict believed in a simple rhythm of day-to-day life, and he ran his monasteries by this belief. The monks under Benedict's care had periods each day for prayer, for work, for eating, for resting. Benedict encouraged his monks to find God in the tilling of the soil, the daily weeding of the garden, and the mundane service in the kitchen. The monastic intentionality of Benedict's life reminds us that sanctity can be found in the simple rhythm of *ora et labora.*

Most people associate monastic life with asceticism—rough robes, hard beds, and midnight prayers in the cold. But while this King of Pentacles is monastic, ascetic he is not. This King lives a simple life, but he is also surrounded by abundance—a safe home, a sunny sky, flora and fauna, a lushness that threatens to spill over the borders of the image. He reminds us that simplicity and asceticism are not one and the same. Benedict believed this, too, and the monks under his care lived surprisingly temperate lives. This was a stark departure from previous monastic sensibility, but Benedict believed more in mercy than severity. To that end, he did not want his monks fasting round the clock, praying all night, or stretching their limits with work. He wanted them to eat well, pray and sleep regularly, work about six hours a day, and take naps when needed.

For Benedict, life was meant to be lived simply, but it was also meant to be celebrated and enjoyed.

The King of Pentacles sits outside the walls of his castle partly because power does not interest him, but also because he wants to share his life with us. The Kings of the tarot are teachers, and Saint Benedict has taught us more about a well-ordered life than perhaps any other saint. Benedict wrote down his monastic rules in the *Rule of Saint Benedict,* and his *Rule* is still read today. It is written in simple language, because Benedict never did anything with complication. Because of that, it is accessible for anyone desiring intimacy with God. Reaching out through his simple words, Benedict of Nursia invites us frazzled, busy, modern folks to embrace a life less complicated. He invites us into *ora et labora,* into an enjoyment of God's good gifts, and into friendship with the Creator who gives us life. To this day, the potent nature of Benedict's life is seen in the quiet muscle of his *Rule* and in those who continue to be inspired by his simple wisdom.

REFLECTIONS

- Are you the kind of person who tries to order your days well, to keep a certain schedule of work and prayer? Do you feel as if that helps you stay close to God? If so, in what ways?
- Reflect on the rhythm of your day-to-day life. Do you find God in each activity of your day? Or only in prayer? Why?
- Spend some time trying to bring prayerful, monastic intentionality to even the smallest tasks of your day:

laundry, dishes, checking email. How do you think it might change you?

- The King of Pentacles is surrounded by abundance. Where can you name abundance in your own life? Can you thank God for that abundance?
- Benedict believed in a devout life, but he also believed in a life of enjoyment. Do you feel as if those two things are mutually exclusive? Why or why not?
- What are some ways in which you can invite a Benedictine spirit of temperance into your life?

PAGE OF SWORDS

Miss no single opportunity of making some small sacrifice, here by a smiling look, there by a kindly word; always doing the smallest right and doing it all for love. (Thérèse of Lisieux)

Saint Thérèse of Lisieux, popularly known as the Little Flower, was a French Carmelite nun who lived in the late nineteenth century. She grew up in a loving and pious home and felt a call to religious life at an early age. Despite persistent health problems, she became a nun at the age of fifteen, entering the cloistered Carmelite community of Lisieux, Normandy, in France, where she spent the remaining nine years of her short life. Thérèse's life was a small one, but she lived into the smallness in such a way that she is a saint not in spite of the smallness of her life but precisely because of it. Thérèse's glory lies in the little things, and her life shows us one way in which the modest but mighty spirit of the Page of Swords can manifest in the world.

The Page of Swords stands on a hill, grasping his sword with a determined look. He holds within himself a willingness to fight, to make himself vulnerable, to suffer for what he loves. He has a bold soul. That being said, he also wears no armor and rides no horse and sits on no throne. Thérèse, too, had this willing spirit of sacrifice stuffed inside the confines of a very small life. Thérèse did not fight the tight boundaries of her life, though, and her holiness lies in the way she leaned into the small sacrifices with fierce determination. We see this outlook most profoundly in her simple approach to the spiritual life, which she called the Little Way. This Little Way centered on a belief that one does not have to do great things in order to become a saint, that sanctity can also be found in the accumulation of small things. Thérèse lived her whole life in daily little sacrifices of love, and all those little sacrifices led her straight to sainthood.

While the sacrifices are small, there is big joy to be found in them. In the Page of Swords, we see neither resentment over the smallness of his life nor grumbling over the sacrifices he makes. The Page of Swords offers himself willingly, and in that sacrificial love he finds joy. Saint Thérèse was no different. She was a joyful saint, and she was joyful not in spite of her little life and her Little Way but because of it. She was utterly devoted to her small sacrifices, acts as modest as offering a smile instead of a harsh comment, or not grumbling when served food she didn't like, and they united her with the great sacrifice of Christ's love for us. Thérèse was so deeply connected to the love of Christ through her daily examples of sacrifice that she was able to live a life of deep joy even amid the steady decline of her health. In her autobiography, she wrote of how the love of God filled her heart to the brim, so that suffering simply skimmed the surface and did not penetrate. In the depths of her heart lived a contentment that could not be disturbed.

Saints who do grand things are a gift, of course, and can inspire us to grandness. The truth, though, is that most of us live perfectly ordinary lives, and we sometimes need reminders that sainthood can also be found in the everyday. The Page of Swords does not stand on a battlefield, but he still wields a sword. He is unlikely to change the world, but his actions still matter. This is what Thérèse and her Little Way gently call us to remember. Christ calls us not to ambition, but to love, and Thérèse's Little Way offers us a guide for performing the sacrificial love of the suit of Swords in our own daily lives. Thérèse wished to be a "strewer of roses," bringing sweetness and joy to all people she met in simple and tangible ways, with kind words and gentle gestures. She reminds us that while Christianity is built on the blood of martyrs, it is kept alive by the flowers of little acts of sacrifice.

REFLECTIONS

- Reflect on Thérèse's Little Way. In what ways can you invite that spirit of little sacrifice into your day?
- The suit of Swords teaches us about suffering, and it's so dramatic that it can sometimes feel inaccessible to us. Do you feel like the Page of Swords' emphasis on small sacrifices helps the sacrificial love seen throughout the suit of Swords feel more attainable? Why or why not?

- The Page of Swords feels joy in his willingness to suffer for what he loves. How can you bring that eager spirit into your own life?
- Thérèse believed that Christ loved the small sacrifices just as much as the big ones. Can you ask God to help you take as much pleasure in your small sacrifices as Christ does? In what ways do you think that might bring more spiritual meaning to your daily life?
- Do you feel like you have the same willing spirit of sacrifice as Thérèse and the Page of Swords? If not, how can you cultivate that?
- How can you be a "strewer of roses" for the people you encounter in your daily life?

KNIGHT OF SWORDS

I do not fear men-at-arms; my way has been made plain before me. If there be men-at-arms my Lord God will make a way for me to go to my Lord Dauphin. For that am I come. (Joan of Arc)

Joan of Arc was born in the French village of Domrémy-la-Pucelle circa 1412. As a young girl, she received mystical visions from the Archangel Michael, Saint Margaret, and Saint Catherine, and in these visions, she was told that it was her destiny to save France by restoring Charles VII to the throne. She led several swift victories for the French before being captured and handed over to the English, who put her on trial, declared her guilty of heresy, and burned her at the stake at the age of nineteen. Joan's short life was characterized by her single-mindedness, her confidence, and her deep belief that she was born to save her country. A young virgin dressed as a soldier and leading armies into battle, she is a saint who has, in some ways, become bigger than herself and taken on the mantle of myth.

The Knights of the tarot live in the white-hot primacy of life, eager and straightforward in most everything they do, and we see this in the way the Knight of Swords charges swiftly into battle with little subtlety. This Knight is characterized by his immediacy, and he shares this trait with Joan of Arc. Joan was not a simple person, but she did carry with her a certain simplicity of purpose. She believed that it was her destiny to save France, and everything she did was aimed toward that goal. Nothing stopped her— neither her gender nor her class, neither threat of torture nor fear of death. She believed that she was an agent of God's will, and she would not let anyone convince her to the contrary. She followed her visions to the very end, and the sheer charisma of this is what led people to follow her. Joan was a cocked arrow, and once she was let loose, nothing stopped her.

This swift ferocity underscores Joan's divinely inspired confidence, and we see this in the Knight of Swords as well. There is no meekness about either of them, and this almost foolhardy courage shone through in nearly every aspect of Joan's life. In the few battles she led before she was captured, she always insisted on a direct strike; to be stealthy was to imply a mistrust in God's abilities. She was obviously not a tactician, but men trusted her confidence all the same; Joan gathered whole armies about her, men who would fanatically follow her anywhere. Even after being captured by the English, her confidence in her mission never wavered. The voices she heard told her to "take everything peacefully" and "have no care for thy martyrdom." And that's what she did. An entire roomful of scheming men could not ruffle her, and she only told them what she wanted to tell, even under threat of torture. Like the Knight of Swords, she was too confident to fear death: she had a destiny to fulfill and God on her side.

Arthur Waite, the cocreator of the Waite-Smith deck, associated the Knight of Swords with Galahad, an Arthurian knight of utmost chastity and purity of heart who found the Holy Grail because of his virtue. Because of this association, there's a sort of mythic quality to the Knight of Swords, and we see this in Joan of Arc's life as well. For generations before Joan appeared on the world's stage, there had been prophecies in France that the country would be restored by a virgin. And then there she was—a young virgin sent by God to save France, the answer to a prophecy's prayers. Legends say that clouds of butterflies followed her wherever she went. She had a high tolerance for physical injury, which was unnatural enough to inspire rumors of superhuman strength. When she was set afire at the stake, the stories tell us that her heart never burned. Joan's life abounds with these moments of myth, and to reduce or erase them would be to do her a disservice. Like the Knight of Swords, her sword was swift because her heart was pure, and she's become mythical because she deserves to be.

REFLECTIONS

- What in your life do you fear? How can you place trust in God's hands as Joan did?
- Joan of Arc was not afraid to upend the status quo in order to fulfill her mission from God. Are you called to do the same? How?
- Tarot's Knights are the most courageous of the court cards. How can you have courage in the face of suffering, as Joan did?

- God gives us each a purpose in life, and Joan was unflinching in pursuit of her purpose. What are some ways in which you can identify and carry out your own purpose for God?
- Do you like to rush into things as the Knight of Swords does, or do you like to plan ahead? Do you think there's a place for both of these personalities in the Kingdom of God? Why or why not?
- What feelings come up when you reflect on the more mythical aspects of Joan's life? Faith? Skepticism? Why?

QUEEN OF SWORDS

He said not "Thou shalt not be tempested, thou shalt not be travailed, thou shalt not be diseased"; but he said, "Thou shalt not be overcome." (Julian of Norwich)

We know so little about Julian of Norwich that not even her name is entirely certain to us; in her writings she does not tell us her real name, and it could be that she simply adopted the name of the church, St. Julian's, where she lived as an anchoress. What we do know is that she was born in England in the fourteenth century and that she lived during a time marked by war, famine, sickness, and unrest. Plague racked her town more than once before she even came to adulthood. Julian grew up amid death, and this closeness to suffering colored her life. It colored the things she asked God for, it colored the visions she was given, and it likely colored her eventual decision to become an anchoress. Julian spent her life trying, in her own way, to make meaning of the world of suffering in which she lived. Her strange visions and the teachings that came out of them touched, and continue to touch, people far beyond her small and lowly cell in Norwich.

The Queen of Swords has no fear of suffering. Indeed, she lifts her hand and invites it to come closer. She desires a closeness to suffering because she desperately wants to understand it. Julian tells us that, as a young woman, she asked God for three things. She asked to have an intimate knowledge of Christ's passion, a sensual recollection of what it would have been like to suffer as Christ suffered. She asked to have a bodily sickness in which she would come as close to death as possible without actually dying. And she asked for three mystical wounds, which she called, "true contrition, . . . genuine compassion, and . . . sincere longing for God." These desires can seem strange to modern ears; most of us would rather shield ourselves from suffering than welcome it in an effort to understand it. But Julian loved Christ enough to want to suffer with him in what she called "fellow-suffering." She took Christlike compassion to its natural theological end, asking to live out Christ's passion with him. Like the Queen of Swords, Julian was no stranger to pain—her life was wholly marked by it—and she wanted to find God there.

The Queen of Swords bravely beckons the suffering forward, and the suffering comes. Sometime around the age of thirty, Julian got her wish. She succumbed to a severe and mysterious illness, and in the midst of this strange sickness, she began to have visions. The priest who came to give her last rites held a cross in front of her face, and in Julian's mind, the cross began to bleed.

Christ's Passion came alive for her, and over the next several hours, she had a series of fifteen visions. In these visions, which alternated between joy and sorrow, Julian saw things like Christ's blood flowing through heaven and hell and earth, the Devil being defeated by Christ's death, Christ's body slowly decaying on the cross, and the pleasure Christ felt at having suffered for her sake. For contemporary readers, the visceral nature of these visions can seem so off-putting as to be almost impenetrable. Julian wanted this, though. She desired to feel the full pain of Christ on the cross in solidarity with both the suffering of Christ and the suffering of humanity, and the nature of that particular suffering changed her life.

While the Queen of Swords calls suffering to her, she does not believe in suffering for suffering's sake. And while she is a mystic, like all the Queens of the tarot, neither is she a mystic for mysticism's sake. The Queen of Swords, with her crown of butterflies, shows us how suffering can be transformed, and Julian of Norwich shows us the same. Julian spent twenty years meditating on the visions she received that night, and what she found was that the suffering of Christ on the cross was unlike the suffering of the plague or the other horrors she had known. It was not an empty black hole of despair, but the suffering of compassion. It was not meaningless pain, but the pain of unfathomable love. Every pain of our lives is suffered also by a God who loves us beyond measure. Life often feels like one long, hard struggle, but our suffering is transformed by our belief in a God who knows exactly what our suffering feels like. The love is greater than the suffering itself. No matter what happens in this life, God holds us in our pain, and so, in the end, "all shall be well, and all shall be well, and all manner of things shall be well."

REFLECTIONS

- Spend some time with the Queen of Swords. How does she seem to you? Brave? Compassionate? Distant? Intense?
- Reflect on the idea that Julian asked for suffering in solidarity with Christ's suffering. Does that seem absurd to you? Can you imagine yourself asking to share in the suffering of Christ on the cross? Why or why not?
- Think of a time in your life in which you experienced suffering. Do you feel as if God was with you in that suffering, as Christ was with Julian of Norwich? Why or why not?
- In *Revelations of Divine Love,* Julian compared Christ's suffering on the cross to a woman in labor. Do you think a maternal view of Christ might broaden your beliefs about Christ's love for you? If so, in what ways?
- Have you ever felt compassionate suffering for someone you love? What was that like for you?
- Do you feel like taking a more mystical view of suffering, like the Queen of Swords does, might help you in your day-to-day struggles? Why or why not?

KING OF SWORDS

Take, Lord, and receive all my liberty, my memory, my understanding, and all my will—all that I have and possess. You, Lord, have given all to me. To you, Lord, I now return it. All is yours. (Ignatius of Loyola)

Ignatius of Loyola, the great sixteenth-century Spanish saint, always knew he was destined for greatness. Born at the castle of Loyola in Spain, he spent his youth as a page in service to a relative, dreaming of military glory. Those dreams were dashed early on, but he managed a glorious legacy all the same, founding a religious order called the Society of Jesus, whose members are focused on missionary and teaching work, and becoming a gifted spiritual director. The simple clarity of Ignatius's spirituality continues to inspire today. He is revered not so much for what he did but for how he allowed God to do great work through him, for how he bent his own will to God's will, and for how he teaches us to do the same.

The King of Swords has great wisdom, but since the suit of Swords tells us about spiritual struggle, we can guess that his wisdom is hard-won. We see this hunch played out in the life of Saint Ignatius. As a young man, Ignatius had no interest in religion. His faith lay not in the Gospels but in the romantic and chivalrous stories of the knights of Camelot and El Cid. That all changed, though, and the catalyst for that change was one fateful day in 1521. While fighting in the Battle of Pamplona, Ignatius was struck by a shot that shattered his right leg. He endured multiple surgeries, which saved his leg but ended his dazzling military career; he walked with a limp for the rest of his life. During his long recovery, he spent months with only *The Imitation of Christ* by Thomas à Kempis and biographies of the saints for company. Confined to his bed, he went inward. He thought about the earthly glory of El Cid and the heavenly glory of Christ. He thought about the adventures of his knights and the adventures of the saints. He thought about what gave him purpose and what did not. What he realized during this time changed his life.

Conversion is a thing with which the King of Swords is intimately familiar. Butterflies, a symbol of transformation, adorn his throne. He knows what it feels like to change one's life in a dramatic way, to begin painfully anew. Ignatius allowed the loss of his military career to change him for the better, taking his suffering and letting it convert him. During his long and painful recovery, Ignatius became keenly attuned to his interior life, learning to recognize which feelings brought him closer to God's will and which feelings had the opposite effect. He realized that when he was close to God's will, he felt a deep interior peace, and he was willing to change his life to keep close to that peace. Like the King of Swords, Ignatius was a sharp and focused man, and he took all of that sharpness and focus and used it to bend his will to the will of God. He offered his entire self not to the glory of the battlefield but to the glory of Christ.

The King of Swords might be intense and wise, but he does not have his head in the clouds. He is a practical fellow, and Ignatius was no different. Out of his deep interior discernment, Ignatius created a set of Christian meditations and prayers called *The Spiritual Exercises*. In their original form, *The Spiritual Exercises* are meant to be completed during a thirty-day retreat of silence and solitude. Each week, retreatants are invited to contemplate the various events in the life of Christ and bring them alive, then to ask themselves how they feel about this great mystery. What is it saying? What is the correct response to that love? Where can courage be found here? For Ignatius, the ultimate purpose of *The Spiritual Exercises* was to discover God's will and then to bend to it, to follow Christ whatever the cost. Ignatius's life and his *Spiritual Exercises* teach us to choose God's will always, even when it hurts.

REFLECTIONS

- Do you feel as if your own moments of suffering have been a catalyst for big life changes? Why or why not?
- For Ignatius, something good came out of his suffering. Do you feel as if it's possible for you to think of suffering in this way? As if something beautiful can grow from the ashes of a life? Why or why not?

- Reflect on the idea of following God's will instead of your own. How does that feel for you?
- Do you have an intentional relationship with your interior self? If not, in what ways do you think that might help you become closer to God?
- Do you feel peace when your own will is united with God's will? Or do you prefer to stick to your own plans? Why?
- Ignatius lived a life of deep courage. Do you also feel willing to follow God no matter the cost? Or do you shy away from such intensity? Why or why not?

PAGE OF CUPS

See what love the Father has given us, that we should
be called children of God; and that is what we are.
(John the Beloved; 1 John 3:1)

John the Beloved spent his whole life as the youngest of the bunch. As a child, he grew up in the shadow of James, his older brother. As an adult, he was the youngest of the twelve apostles. Perhaps this is what gave John his youthfulness of spirit, that particular gift of his. Jesus tells us that we must become like children to enter the kingdom of heaven, and John is a perfect example of this advice in action. John loved Jesus with a shocking purity of heart. His entire life hinged on his deliberate belief and active acceptance of the lavish love of God. Known specifically as the "disciple whom Jesus loved" (John 21:7), he was impulsive and affectionate, and he clung to Christ above all, the way a child clings to his mother. And in John's youthful love, we see a glimpse of something we too can learn.

In his hand, the Page of Cups holds a cup from which emerges a little fish. It is a silly and surprising thing, but the Page seems charmed by the surprise. There is no shock, only delight. Like the ocean behind him, he rolls along with it. When we look at John's life, we see this same willingness to be charmed. In the famous story from the Gospels, Jesus calls John to be a fisher of men, and John drops everything to follow Jesus. Jesus offers his love, and John accepts without hesitation. He does not side-eye Jesus. He does not ask questions. He does not request some time to think about it. He allows himself to be surprised by Christ's love, even when it seems strange or odd or unimaginable. With the unself-consciousness of a child, John was willing to jump into Christ's love even when it seemed foolish. John did not ask for Jesus, but Jesus asked for John, and John allowed himself to accept the marvel of it.

The Page of Cups wears a tunic decorated with lotus blossoms, a symbol of purity. This Page is wholly guileless in the way a child is. He wants to love and be loved, nothing more and nothing less. It is easy to see this same innocent spirit in John. When John dropped everything to follow Jesus, Jesus quickly became the center of John's world. Almost achingly pure of heart, John's only aim in life was to be close to Jesus, and he got his wish. He was one of only a few apostles who was present with Jesus in intimate places like the Mount of Transfiguration and the resurrection chamber of Jairus's daughter. He sat at Jesus's side at the Last Supper. He was present at the crucifixion, the only apostle brave enough to be there. John was willing to follow Jesus anywhere, even when staying close meant watching Jesus die, and in this instinctual closeness we see the purest desire to love.

The Page of Cups is interested in love, but he is not interested in grand gestures or playing the hero. For him, devotion counts for more than distinction. This simplicity was present in John's life as well. We know virtually nothing about John's ministry after the life of Jesus. He was not a great missionary like Paul. He was not the rock on which Christ built his church like Peter. He was not heroically martyred like James or Andrew. All we know is that John lived for a long time in relative obscurity. The obscurity is the point, though. John did not need to be a hero. Even the Gospel he wrote was penned anonymously in order to keep the focus, as always, on divine love. All John wanted, in his whole life, was to be a child of God. Others may have lived grander lives, but John was always John the Beloved, and who could want more than that?

REFLECTIONS

- The Page of Cups believes that his purpose in life is to love and be loved by God. What if that was your purpose as well? What if it was your only purpose? Does it feel like enough?
- Reflect on the goals and aspirations you have for your life. Does love factor into them? If not, how might it change your life to center love in that way?
- Do you feel like you let yourself be surprised by the love of Christ? Or are you suspicious of it? What do you think might happen if you let God delight you?
- When do you feel close to Jesus as John the Beloved did? How can you cultivate more moments like that in your life?

- John the Beloved's life is a reminder that God does not need grand gestures of love from us, that God is happy with our mere presence. What are some small ways in which you can express your love for God? How can you help yourself believe that God is just as happy with the small expressions of love?
- We like to make love complicated, but both the Page of Cups and John the Beloved are delightfully uncomplicated in their love. Reflect on this. Do you feel like love is a simple thing? Or does it feel complicated to you? Why?

KNIGHT OF CUPS

In the dark night of the soul, bright flows the river of God. (John of the Cross)

John of the Cross was a Spanish priest, especially gifted as a spiritual director and confessor. He was a mystic, having visions of Christ crucified. He was a reformer, working with Saint Teresa of Ávila to found a new monastery for Carmelite friars. Above all, though, John was a poet, one of the greatest poets of the Christian tradition. In true poetic spirit, John was a man who believed that what was happening in our souls was just as important as what was happening in the outside world. As dramatic as his outward life was, his interior life was even more so, and his poems and commentary on them leave us a record of this. No matter what John did in his day-to-day life, his soul was always seeking God, and his poems teach us how to seek as well. They are perhaps his greatest gift to us.

The Knight of Cups is grace personified. The cup he holds calls to mind the chivalrous grail-seeking knights of Arthurian legend. The stance of the horse he rides is reminiscent of the lovely dancing Andalusian horses of Spain. The Knight's tunic is decorated with little fish, that symbol of Christ. He is a true romantic, seeking his Beloved, and the heart he's trying to win is Christ's own. We see this same graceful, romantic spirit in the life of John of the Cross. John believed that the whole of the spiritual life is nothing more and nothing less than this romantic seeking for God. We see this reflected in much of his poetry. The *Spiritual Canticle,* a sort of Spanish rewrite of the Song of Songs, is about a shepherdess searching for the shepherd whom she loves. It is widely considered to be a masterpiece of Spanish poetry, and it is a love story that reflects John's own. John was the shepherdess seeking the shepherd, the Bride looking for the Bridegroom, the lover seeking Christ's love.

The Knight of Cups is seeking his Beloved, and he is doing so in an inhospitable landscape. He is made for water—he holds a cup and his tunic is decorated with small fish—but he is wandering in a desert. This is the most severe landscape we see in the suit of Cups, but the Knight is here willingly. Like all the Knights of the tarot, he is no stranger to struggle, and he never shies from a challenge. We know this is also true of John, whose best-known work is the dramatically named "Dark Night of the Soul." This poem and accompanying commentary describes the painful spiritual struggle of attempting union with the Beloved. This dark night of the soul is a spiritual desert. It is a period of desolation and lostness. It is a time when everything that is not God is purged from the soul, and it hurts. It takes great courage to enter into this emptiness of spirit and move through it instead of run away, but John was as willing as the Knight of Cups is here.

The Knight wanders in a desert, but he is not unhappy. He smiles, and he looks at his chalice, that symbol of God's love. He knows that God is in the desert, too, and he knows that he will find his Beloved. John found God in his own spiritual desert. Christ entered and revealed his presence in the dark night of John's heart. John, ever the poet, shows us the blessing in the struggle of the dark night. What John learned, and what John teaches us, is that in the desert, the soul is stripped of all desires that are not of God. What John teaches us is that we can learn to find peace in the dark night, because it is the place where nothing exists except God. What John teaches us is that the river of God flows brightly, even in the deserts of the heart.

REFLECTIONS

- Saint John of the Cross had a deeply romantic relationship with God. Reflect on this idea. How does it feel to think of your own relationship with God as a romantic one?
- John was, first and foremost, a poet. Do you feel like you can connect with God through poetry? Or does your relationship with God take a more logical approach? Why?
- Is your faith more inward focused or outward focused? (There's no right or wrong answer here!) How does that manifest in your life?
- Have you ever experienced a dark night of the soul? If so, what was it like for you?
- Both John of the Cross and the Knight of Cups see the inner life as an adventure worth paying attention

to. Do you feel that way about your own inner life, as a landscape worth exploring? Why or why not?

- John believed that the river of God flows brightly even in the dark night of the soul. How might that change your perspective on spiritual struggle, to believe that God can be found even in the deserts?

QUEEN OF CUPS

God withholds Himself from no one who perseveres.
(Teresa of Ávila)

In popular culture, mystics are often portrayed as somewhat aloof characters, so wrapped up in their interior worlds that they shut themselves off from other people, becoming detached and distant. That popular portrayal has its place, but Teresa of Ávila, that great Spanish mystic, shows us something altogether different. Teresa was anything but aloof. Warm and charming, she laughed and laughed often. She loved the world, and she loved people, and she loved being in love. Teresa's mysticism grew out of this warm and loving personality. She was a mystic not in spite of but *because* of this love of the world, this deeply human desire to love and be loved. She had a vast longing in her human heart, satisfied only by God, and her life shows us what an intimate relationship with the Beloved can be.

The Queen of Cups sits on a throne decorated with tiny mermaids and a curved scallop shell, calling to mind Venus, the goddess of love. More than any other court card, the Queen of Cups has an instinctual longing for beauty and romance. Teresa was much the same. She became a Carmelite nun at the age of twenty, but the decision had less to do with an ardent calling to religious life and more to do with not wanting to be married. She was an ambivalent nun, at least at the start. While Teresa wanted to be devout, for many years her inner life was dry and tedious, and prayer inspired little feeling in her. She wanted to want God, but in the absence of that desire, being well-liked by other people filled its place. Endowed with natural beauty, charm, intelligence, and humor, Teresa used the attentions of other people as a way to satisfy her desire for love, to fill the empty love-longing space in her heart.

The Queen of Cups sits on her throne of beauty right at the edge of a sea. Her blue robe mimics the eddies of the sea so well that it is difficult to tell where she ends and the sea begins. While she is not in the ocean itself, she is close enough to touch it. She is curious and open and willing to let herself be transformed by it. Teresa had this same willingness of spirit. She had a heart made for love, and the attentions of other people never quite satisfied her. She wanted the vast ocean of God's love badly enough to stand on the edge and wait for it. She prayed even when it felt meaningless, as it did for a long time. She continued in her religious life, even when it felt pointless and inconsequential. Teresa lived with trust and a willingness to be changed, and eventually God changed her. She opened her heart again and again, and eventually God flooded it with boundless love.

Sitting on her lovely Venusian throne, the Queen of Cups gazes at what is the most elaborate of the cups we see in the suit of Cups. It is, in fact, not a normal cup but a ciborium, a special container that holds the consecrated hosts eaten during communion. What the Queen of Cups gazes at with deep devotional tenderness is the Eucharist. The only love grand enough to satisfy Teresa's love-longing was divine love, and once divine love made its presence felt, Teresa fell head over heels. She began to have visions, the most famous of which is the transverberation, where an angel pierced her heart with a golden arrow, leaving her in ecstasy. In the wake of these visions, the pleasures of the world were no longer satisfying. Her instinct for beauty was sated only in God. Her desire for love was satisfied only by the Beloved. Her openheartedness was rewarded by the love to end all loves.

REFLECTIONS

- Both the Queen of Cups and Teresa of Ávila are very romantic characters. Do you relate to this? Does faith feel romantic for you? Why or why not?
- Teresa was a naturally engaging and charming woman. Do you feel as if this is a gift of yours as well? If so, how can you use that gift to draw closer to God?
- Teresa struggled with a years-long period of "dryness of soul," a feeling that God was far away from her. Have you ever experienced this? If so, were you able to maintain an openness to God as Teresa did?
- Have you ever struggled, as Teresa did, with looking to other people to give you the kind of love only God can give? If so, what was that like for you?

- When you think about mystics, what kind of personality comes to mind? Does Teresa's passionate and extroverted character challenge your perceptions? If so, in what ways?
- Reflect on the Queen of Cups' focused gaze on the Eucharist. Who or what in your life receives that kind of attention and loving focus? Is it God? Or something else?

KING OF CUPS

Love and affection have a greater empire over souls than harshness and severity. Love is more powerful than the strongest arguments, the most convincing reasons. (Francis de Sales)

We know, as Christians, that we are called to love others the way Christ loved us. We know that we are supposed to love every person we meet with gentleness, with openheartedness, with grace. What does that look like in practice, though? Well, it looks a lot like the life of Francis de Sales. Francis turned loving others into an art form. He had a deep faith rooted in the love of God, and his belief in God's unending love showed in the softness with which he interacted with other people. During his life, he worked to heal the religious divisions in France at the time, showing people what it looked like to be loved by God and to love in turn. Many saints are bold and contentious, and there is a place in heaven for those personalities, but Francis shows us a different side of sainthood. His gentle and encouraging approach to spirituality encourages us even today.

The King of Cups sits on the simplest throne of any in the court cards. What is unusual about it is not its design but that it seems to be placed directly in the middle of the sea. Rather than staying in one place, the King of Cups floats along on the swell of the waves. He is moved by them, letting them take him where they may, and his expression is serene and clear-eyed. Francis de Sales was this way, too, living in the ocean of God's love and carried along by its currents. He always let divine love guide him, even when it took him to unusual places. This divine love is what carried Francis to the priesthood, a vocation he certainly would not have chosen himself. He was born into a noble family, offered a privileged education, and was expected to become a magistrate. Instead, Francis renounced the life of comfort and ease that was his birthright and devoted his life to God's service.

The King of Cups is a bit paradoxical in that he is a king without a land to rule. He has no interest in claiming authority over people, and neither did Francis de Sales. Francis had no earthly ambition. He renounced his noble life to become a priest. While he became a bishop later in life, he did so out of obedience rather than desire. Swimming around in a sea of God's love, what Francis most desired was to lead other people to that same love. He did this not with an iron fist but with a gentle hand. This gentleness drew people to him; he became known as a great confessor and spiritual director because his mere presence was so comforting. Like the King of Cups, he was never above people but always *with* them, always making himself gently accessible to whomever needed him. Everything he did, he did in love.

Like all the Kings of the tarot, the King of Cups is a teacher and a guide. He wants to lead other people to the love he knows so well, and his reach is as vast as the endless sea that surrounds him. During his life, Frances de Sales led a great number of people to God, but his influence stretches beyond his earthly life. As a saint, Francis is perhaps most well-known for his writings on spiritual formation. He wrote two books in particular that are pillars of the Christian faith: *Treatise on the Love of God* and *Introduction to the Devout Life*. These books teach us about, respectively, the love of God and how to live in the love of God. Suffused with Francis's trademark gentleness and sincerity, their language is so clear and beautiful that it cuts straight to the heart. Through these writings, Francis continues to guide us to divine love and to show us how to guide others to that love.

REFLECTIONS

- Do you feel like you have an easy time following God's love wherever it might take you? Or do you resist it? Why?
- Francis felt deeply connected to God's love, and this helped to guide his life. Do you feel connected to God's love in your day-to-day life? If so, how do you let that love guide your decision-making?
- Think about the people in your life who have led you to God. What were they like? Angry? Peaceful? Stern? Kind?
- Is there anyone in your life who you feel embodies the gentle spirit of Francis de Sales and the King of Cups? If so, what are they like to be around?

- Francis de Sales, like the King of Cups, always looked to serve others rather than rule over them. Do you feel like you're good at cultivating that spirit of servanthood? If not, how do you think it might change your life to concern yourself more with lifting up others rather than lifting up yourself?
- Francis de Sales expressed his love, in part, through his spiritual writings. How do you express your love for others? How does divine love shine through you?

PAGE OF WANDS

Let us strive after purity of heart, for the Holy Spirit
dwells in candid and simple minds. (Philip Neri)

Born in Florence in 1515, Philip Neri was a charming boy who
grew into a charming man. The patron saint of joy and laughter,
Philip's great gift was this supernatural charm. He did not prophesy or evangelize or perform great miracles, but he had mirth and
good humor in spades, and he led people to God by simply being
the kind of person one wants to be around. His genius was his
candid and unassuming joy, and he used this genius to minister
to the people of Rome, day in and day out. He and the Page of
Wands remind us that we need not be megavisionaries in order to
let the Holy Spirit move in our lives, that joy is as potent a fruit of
the Spirit as any other.

All the Pages live small lives, keen to find sanctity in the day-to-day, and the Page of Wands is no different. Despite his enthusiastic nature, he lives small, and we see this idea played out in Philip Neri's life. Philip's spirit was apostolic in its zeal, and as a youth he wished to go to the Indies to be a missionary. Unlike many of the great saints of his era, though, Philip found that his vocation was to a single city. He had the fervent enthusiasm of a missionary, but his mission was not across the world. His mission was Rome. He spent his life converting and sanctifying souls there through so many little tasks: preaching in marketplaces, hearing confessions, caring for the sick, ministering to needy pilgrims. There was enough that needed doing in Rome, and he felt that saving souls close to home was as pleasing to God as saving them anywhere else. He was a visionary, but his vision was concentrated on one place.

The Page of Wands might live a small life, but it is no less fervent for that. From his tunic adorned with salamanders—mythically associated with fire—to the lick-of-fire feather in his cap, he tells us of passion. Philip was no stranger to this passion, a trait that is best illustrated by one particular story. Philip always had a special devotion to the Holy Spirit, and one night, while he was praying for the Holy Spirit's gifts and graces, he saw a globe of fire appear in front of him. The globe of fire entered his mouth and sank down into his heart. At the moment this happened, he felt within him what he described as a fire of love that manifested as an actual physical heat. Philip was not frightened by this; on the contrary, he felt an extraordinary sense of supernatural joy. When he put his hand to his heart, he felt a swelling as big as a man's fist. For the remainder of his life, he had regular heart palpitations that occurred when he prayed, as if the fervor of the Holy Spirit could not be contained in his body.

That fervor spills out of the Page of Wands, and because the

Pages are so childlike, it reveals itself mostly as joy. In true Page of Wands fashion, the distinctive mark of Philip's life was a youthful cheerfulness. His room in Rome was affectionately known as the School of Christian Mirth. He had such an extraordinary joy that it interfered with the practicalities of his daily life: when preparing for mass, he would often become so excited that he had to have frivolous books read to him in order to ground him enough to move through the necessary rituals. The gift of this supernatural joy was obviously captivating, and Philip used this great personal charm to his advantage, leading people to God with it. He was so affectionate that he drew all of Rome with him, and through this example, he kindled in others the fire of the love of God with which he himself burned.

REFLECTIONS

- Do you believe that the Holy Spirit can move in our lives in small ways? Or only in big ways? Why?
- Both the Page of Wands and Philip Neri are visionaries, but their visions are small ones. Does this appeal to you? Or do you think of visionaries as necessarily thinking big-picture? What would it look like to be a visionary in a small-scale way?
- Philip Neri's life reminds us that joy is a fruit of the Spirit. Do you associate the work of the Holy Spirit with joy? Does it make you happy to do God's work in the world? Why or why not?
- Both Philip Neri and the Page of Wands are not only joyful, but funny and charming. Do you think of holy people as being warm and gregarious? Or do you

always picture them as being serious and intellectual? Why?

- Philip prayed for the Holy Spirit's gifts, and, like a child, trusted that he would receive them. Do you pray for the Holy Spirit's gifts? Do you trust that, if you ask, you will receive? If so, how does that inspire your faith?
- Philip brought people to God by remaining deeply in touch with the joy of Christian life. When you talk with people about Christianity, does that joy feel palpable? Why or why not?

KNIGHT OF WANDS

I am the voice of one crying out in the wilderness, "Make straight the way of the Lord." (John the Baptist; John 1:23)

In the Gospels, Jesus proclaimed, "Among those born of women no one has arisen greater than John the Baptist" (Matthew 11:11). He wasn't wrong. John the Baptist's whole life was a bright and burning marvel. Along with Jesus, he is one of only two people in history whose birth was foretold by the prophets and announced by the angels. The purpose of his life was to be a prophet himself, proclaiming the blazing glory of the coming of a Savior and making sure that people were ready to receive said Savior. He was made to prepare a way between the old world and the world to come, and he fulfilled this calling with fervor and dedication and clear-eyed singleness of purpose. A voice crying out in the wilderness, John held aloft the prophetic flame, instituted the sacrament of baptism, and readied people for the new world.

One look at the Knight of Wands, with his tunic patterned with salamanders and his armor licked with flames, tells us that he is a man guided by passion. John the Baptist was no different. When an angel came to Elizabeth and Zechariah to announce their son John's birth, the angel declared that John would be filled with the Holy Spirit, and so it was. The Holy Spirit moved through John's life, and John followed. He allowed himself to be guided by this passion even before he was born, famously leaping in the womb in the presence of Jesus. He also allowed himself to be guided by this passion even when it made no sense, choosing to live in the wilderness rather than follow in the priestly footsteps of his father. It was through this deep trust in the Spirit that John became John as we know him best, a desert-dwelling man wearing a camel coat and living on locusts and honey, a refiner's fire burning brightly enough within him for people to take notice.

The Knight of Wands charges ahead on a rearing warhorse. He has an urgent message, and he commands that people take notice and listen. John, the great prophet, moved through the world with that same urgency. The angel who foretold John's birth said that John would go forth in spirit to make ready the people for the Lord, and John did. Like the Knight of Wands, he was a forerunner with a powerful and enduring message, and his message was this: make way for the Lord. John spent his earthly ministry telling anyone who would listen that the kingdom of heaven was at hand and that lives should change accordingly. Many people did listen; John was a difficult man to ignore. Under his influence, the way of the Lord was paved by lives changed and hearts turned to God. John instituted the sacrament of baptism as an outward sign of those inward changes of the heart, and as the culmination of his role as prophet, he baptized Jesus himself.

To be so passionate—to be such a prophet—necessitates courage. Luckily, the Knight of Wands has courage to spare, and so did John the Baptist. Prophecy is a dangerous vocation, but John was never one to shy away from a task, no matter how risky. A prophet has a dual role of predicting the future and speaking difficult truths, and John did both without fear. He said what the Holy Spirit compelled him to say, even if it brought him into real danger and made him sometimes uncomfortable to be around. He was willing to be a voice crying out in the wilderness, even when it came at great cost. John was the first prophet of the New Testament, but he was also its first martyr, famously beheaded at the request of Herod's daughter Salome. He gave his life to prepare the way, and he shows us what can happen when one bold voice is willing to risk a cry in the wilderness.

REFLECTIONS

- Spend some time reflecting on the life of John the Baptist. Does he feel relatable to you? Or does his life feel too bold and dramatic to be relatable? Why?
- John the Baptist was a great prophet. Do you feel like his words are still relevant today? Do you feel like they're relevant to you, personally? If so, in what ways?
- Spend some time thinking on your own ideas about baptism. How might they connect with John the Baptist and the Knight of Wands and the lessons they teach?

- Very few of us are true prophets, but we can still bring the spirit of the prophets into our lives. What truths feel like yours to speak?
- Do you feel like it's easy for you to be bold and outspoken in the way that John was? If not, can you ask the Holy Spirit to help you? How might that change your life?
- John never minded making people feel uncomfortable with his truth-speaking. Do you feel as if you hold that same courage? Why or why not?

QUEEN OF WANDS

Be who God meant you to be and you will set the world on fire. (Catherine of Siena)

Catherine of Siena was born in 1347, right into the thick of a big, devout family. The eleventh of twelve children, one might expect that she got lost in the shuffle, but even as a young girl, Catherine never let herself be overlooked. She was such a happy child that her family nicknamed her Euphrosyne, Greek for "joy." A happy child is not always an easy child, though, and Catherine was also headstrong, resisting expectations at every turn. Her parents wanted her to marry, as most fourteenth-century parents certainly wished for their daughters, but Catherine refused. Instead, she chose to become a lay Dominican, living a prayerful but active life outside a convent's walls. Catherine accomplished much in her life through fiery outspokenness and sheer force of will, and she reminds us that a woman's place in Christianity need not always be a meek one.

All of the Queens are mystics, and the Queen of Wands is no exception. She is a passionate woman, though, and so there is a particular ardor to her visions. We see this in Catherine of Siena, a woman who was nothing if not intense. A true mystic, she had visions that started when she was a young girl and continued throughout her life. Many of these were embodied, romantic visions of Christ. She had visions wherein Christ taught her how to read and write. She had a vision of her heart being taken out of her body by Christ and replaced with Christ's own, after which her heart would throb when she received the Eucharist. In what is perhaps the most famous of her visions, she gave herself to Christ in mystical marriage, after which she received the stigmata. Catherine was a celibate, but through her many visions she carried on a passionate and spiritually intimate relationship with her Beloved.

The Queen of Wands might be a mystic, but that is not all she is. Indeed, it could not be all she is—she has too fervent a soul to stay hidden away in the confines of an interior life. The same is true for Catherine of Siena. Her visions were fantastical, and that spirit of mysticism spilled out into her active life, the one always informing the other. Catherine lived during a time of much social and political tension, and, never one to keep out of things, she was drawn to intervene in the political life of the Catholic Church. She traveled through Italy advocating for clergy reform. She carried on long correspondences with higher-ups in the Church, including Pope Gregory XI, encouraging him to return the papal seat to Rome from Avignon. She spent much time between Florence and Rome, wielding her considerable influence in an attempt to keep peace between the Papal States. And ever loud and ever head-strong, she did all this with great relish.

In front of the Queen of Wands, at her feet, sits a cat at attention. The cat tells us of the Queen of Wands' fierce streak of independence. Catherine of Siena shared this independence, and it runs like a thread through her whole life, the thing that stitched together every decision she made. During a time when women had the choice of being either a married woman or a nun, Catherine was neither. She stepped outside the bounds of what her life was supposed to be, forging her own path and being exactly what God meant her to be, even when it made other people uncomfortable. She had a voice and she used it, never feeling like it wasn't her place to tell political leaders how to be better leaders, to tell priests how to be better priests, to tell the pope how to be a better pope. In expressing her deep interior passion, Catherine was exactly and perfectly herself, and she set the world on fire.

REFLECTIONS

- Spend some time reflecting on the Queen of Wands and her personality. How does her boldness and self-assurance feel to you? Does it feel off-putting? Inspiring? Why?
- Reflect on your own experiences in church. What were you taught about women and how they should be? Do Saint Catherine and the Queen of Wands push back against those ideas?
- Are there any women in your life who remind you of Saint Catherine or the Queen of Wands? If so, how have they changed your life?

- Do you feel comfortable speaking up in religious settings? Why or why not?
- One of the great lessons of Catherine's life is that one can be a mystic and also be an active presence in the world. Does this change your perception of mysticism? If so, in what ways?
- Catherine of Siena's great gift lay in being exactly who God called her to be, even when it made people uncomfortable or annoyed. Do you feel as if this is a particular gift of yours? If not, how might it change your life to embody that particular kind of courage?

KING OF WANDS

Let us not become weary in doing good, for at the proper time we will reap a harvest if we do not give up. (Paul the Apostle; Galatians 6:9)

We all know Paul the Apostle; Paul the Apostle is a man who demands to be known. Paul was not always Paul, though. He began his life as Saul, and he was a Pharisee who spent his early life zealously persecuting those in the early Christian church. Saul had a dramatic and now-famous conversion on the road to Damascus, seeing a blinding light and speaking directly with the voice of Jesus. Wholly transformed by this experience, he changed his name and abruptly shifted his considerable energy into building up the kingdom of God, rather than viciously tearing it down person by person. Paul was at the forefront of shaping the newly born Christian world, of figuring out what it actually means to be a Christian. A true cocreator with God, Paul shows us what the Holy Spirit looks like in action, and while Paul would never say that he changed the world, he most certainly did.

A contentious and cantankerous man, the King of Wands is perhaps the most overtly headstrong of all the court cards. He does not have an easy personality. What he does have is true zeal, that passion of the Holy Spirit that runs like an electric current through the suit of Wands. Paul was charged with this zeal, too, and while it could be off-putting and overwhelming, it also got things done. Transformed from a zealous persecutor to a zealous apostle, he put his bullheadedness to God's use. Paul was energetic and talkative; he had controversial things to say and he said them. He did not hold back. He did not tone down his message. He was not one for a soft approach. He was blunt and direct, and not everyone liked it. Not everyone likes it still, even two thousand years later. Paul serves as a pressing reminder, though, that hardheadedness does not preclude sainthood.

The King of Wands leans forward with one hand on a thigh as if he can barely stay in his seat. Pulsing with energy, he is not one to sit still and he is not one to rule from a distant throne. Paul was no different. He felt that the coming of Jesus had launched a whole new phase of God's divine plan, and he was determined to be at the forefront of it. Nobody knew what a Christian way of life looked like, and so Paul set out to model it from scratch. He had a seemingly limitless store of energy, and he used it to travel all over the place, moving from Syria through what is now Turkey and Greece and winding his way back to Jerusalem. Everywhere he went, he talked about Jesus as the true Messiah and established little groups of unlikely people bound together by his passionate message. These communities did not stay little—they turned into what became the Christian church.

The King of Wands is a big-picture thinker, as all the Kings are. He has too much raw energy to be anything different, and we see this played out in Paul's life, too. There is, after all, nothing more big-picture than showing the first-century world an entirely new way of life. This outsized influence extends to us even here in the present day. Paul wrote letters to the little communities he built up in cities like Ephesus, Corinth, and Philippi, and these letters make up a large part of our New Testament. In these letters, Paul taught people how to live from the perspective of the new kingdom of heaven. These letters teach us still. They capture Paul's teaching and praying, his arguing and his struggle. Through his words, Paul waits to grab us by the hand and show us what it means to live as a Christian in the world, with all its contradictions and trials, beauties and surprises.

REFLECTIONS

- What do you know about Paul? What have you been taught about him? If your impression of him is one of a brash and unrelenting man, has that colored your perspective on his teachings?
- Do you feel as if you must be meek and mild in order to please God? How might Paul's life and personality change your perspective?
- Reflect on the concept of zeal. Do you feel like a zealous person? If not, would you like to be? What would that look like for you?
- Paul had a lot of energy and he put it to good use. Where does your energy go? How can you focus it toward God?

- Do you have big-picture ideas about the Christian life? If so, do you feel comfortable sharing them? Why or why not?
- How can you cultivate Paul's forward-thinking courage in your own day-to-day life?

ACKNOWLEDGMENTS

To be a first-time author is difficult. To be a first-time author with such an unusual book idea is doubly difficult. Thank you to my agent, Meg Thompson, for believing in this book from the very start and for helping me find a wonderful home for it at St. Martin's Essentials. This book wouldn't exist without you.

Thank you to everyone at St. Martin's Essentials who helped get this book into your hands, with special gratitude to my editor, Gwen Hawkes. I couldn't have dreamed a better editor for this project; thank you for lending your expertise on both tarot and theology, and thank you for all your guidance through my first publishing experience.

I wrote this book during a pandemic, and it couldn't have been done without the help of my in-laws, who provided me with countless hours of childcare and took over remote learning responsibilities for my two sons during the 2020–2021 school year. Thank you, Sandy and John, for letting me drop off my kids at your apartment daily so they could play and learn and so I could write a book knowing they were in safe, loving hands.

It's a common belief that having children hinders a woman's creativity; I have found the opposite to be true. This is, in part, because I'm privileged to have family support, but it's also because my children have taught me so much about myself. So thank you to Elijah and Aubrey, for letting me into your sweet worlds and making me a braver, more interesting, and more creative woman than I was before I had the privilege of mothering you.

Everything in my life that matters to me is wrapped up in my faith. A special thank-you to my parents, James and Laura, who gave me a religion that I get to spend the rest of my life exploring with delight.

Writing a book is a lot easier with a supportive partner in one's corner. Thank you, Alex, for being my constant companion while I wrote this book in our tiny New York apartment, for letting me interrupt your work countless times to procrastinate or talk through an idea, and for so easily finding delight in whatever delights me. I could never love anyone more than I love you.

Lastly, this book owes its very existence to every person who met the idea of it with curiosity instead of condemnation. If you are one of those people, I owe you a debt of gratitude.

INDEX

ABOUT THE AUTHOR

Melanie Applegate

Brittany Muller is a writer, mother, wife, and enthusiastic believer in the beautiful strangeness of Christianity. A devout Catholic with an equally devout sense of curiosity, her favorite pastime is finding new ways to think about God. She lives in Austin with her quiet husband and two lively sons, and if you're ever looking for her, she's probably sitting under a live oak and reading about saints.